Schusters' & Gimbels

MILWAUKEE'S BELOVED DEPARTMENT STORES

[signature]

PAUL H. GEENEN

Charleston — London

THE
History
PRESS

Published by The History Press
Charleston, SC 29403
www.historypress.net

Front cover, top: courtesy of Bud Schneider; *bottom*: courtesy of Milwaukee County
Historical Society.
Back cover, top left: courtesy of Historic Photo Collection/Milwaukee Public Library; *top right*:
courtesy of James Baker Jr.; *bottom*: courtesy of Eric Cappel.

First published 2012

Manufactured in the United States

ISBN 978.1.60949.389.9

Library of Congress CIP data applied for.

Notice: The information in this book is true and complete to the best of our knowledge. It is
offered without guarantee on the part of the author or The History Press. The author and
The History Press disclaim all liability in connection with the use of this book.

This book is dedicated to my wife, Patricia Geenen, whom I met at Geenen's Dry Goods fifty years ago and who has supported and encouraged me ever since.

Contents

Preface

There is a tremendous amount of historical information available about Gimbels and Schuster's. Both companies published employee newsletters, and every issue is on file at the Milwaukee County Historical Society. Much of my information comes from employee newsletters: Schuster's *Keeping In Touch*, later called *K.I.T.*, and the Gimbels employee newsletters, *Broadcaster*, *Gimbelite* and *Front and Forward*. These newsletters contain information about major developments, management's strategies and the work life of the employees at both companies. The Gimbels employee publications editor was probably responsible for the detailed history of Gimbels that was published over a number of years, printed on gold stock and distributed as an insert in various employee publications. These inserts were an important source for this book.

I interviewed people who worked in the stores, merchandise and support departments at Gimbels and Schuster's. These interviews gave me background information that supplemented the information I found in my research. Some of my own experiences from working at Gimbels were included in the book also. I started in 1976 as a buyer and was divisional merchandise manager over the Marketplace before I left in 1983.

I leapt at the opportunity to write this book, as department stores have always been part of my family's DNA. My three great-aunts—Minnie, Dina and Anna Geenen—started a department store in Appleton, Wisconsin, in 1896. The three sisters started their store at a time when women were not considered able to manage on their own. Both my father and my mother

Minnie, Dina and Anna Geenen in the early 1900s. They are founders of Geenen's Dry Goods in Appleton, Wisconsin. *Courtesy of Paul Geenen.*

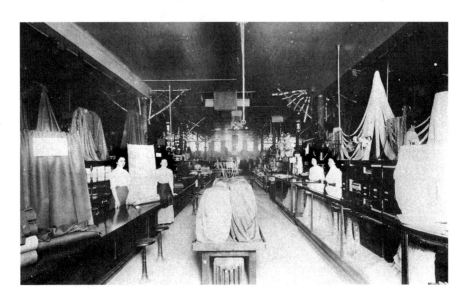

The interior of Geenen's Dry Goods, 1898 or 1900. *Courtesy of Paul Geenen.*

worked at Geenen's Dry Goods for many years. I worked in the store during the summer of my high school and college years and met my wife there. The store closed in 1966.

Time has passed, and events have become clearer. Department stores like to use hyperbole such as "biggest," "most" or "best." Information that could affect business was sometimes swept under the rug. It is now possible to take another look at the history of Gimbels and Schuster's.

Acknowledgements

I wish to thank those who made this book possible, including Harold Badzinski, Irene Baer, Leon Boniface, Francis E. Bryant, Deidra Y.A. Edwards, Priscilla Franklin, Helene Furst, Phyllis Gorell, Mike Hammack, Humanities Department of the Milwaukee Public Library, Dave J. Johnson, Jack A. Koplin, Carol M. Larson, Michael J. Lisicky, Constance E. Little-Whiteside, Clark J. Miller, Milwaukee County Historical Society, Bill Orenstein, Stan Sapiro, Bud Schneider and Robert Schultz.

CHAPTER 1

Two Immigrant German Retailers

1842–1900

GIMBELS

Jacob Gimbel stood at the corner of what is now Wisconsin and Plankinton in 1886 closely observing the traffic that was going by this strategic location. He was the oldest son of seventy-six-year-old Adam Gimbel, the owner of the successful two-and-a-half-story dry goods store in Vincennes, Indiana, called the "Palace of Trade."

Almost half the people walking by were family members of workers employed in Milwaukee's vibrant industrial base of breweries, foundries, tanneries, meatpacking companies and flour mills. Heavy beer wagons carrying twelve barrels—six on each side, each stored at a forty-five-degree angle—were making their deliveries. A tall ship was tied up at the wharf a block east, with its topsails towering over everything. Officers and crews of ships came and went. Sleek horses pulled canopied, large-wheeled carriages.

Women in hoop skirts covering their high-button shoes, African American maids carrying packages for their middle-class matrons, men with derbies, boys with caps and immigrant workers from Eastern European countries were walking on the wide plank sidewalks while wagons filled with hides, beer and meat traversed the rutted dirt street. A scrabble of rocks lined the side of the street, offering pedestrians some means to keep their boots clean from the mud.

Streetcars, powered by newly electrified overhead cables, rode the rails silently, taking advantage of the brand-new power plant built by

Wisconsin Electric Power Company. The twin streetcar lines, creating diamond patterns in the center of the intersection, extended, as John Gurda tells in his book *The Making of Milwaukee*, out to Wauwatosa, North Greenfield and Waukesha. The arched iron swing bridge angled to meet Wisconsin Avenue to the east and allowed wheeled and foot traffic to cross the river.

This was a good corner to sell newspapers, and newsboys with stacks of newspapers under their arms staked out their positions as soon as the papers came off the press. Men sitting straight and tall on bicycles peddled by slowly to maintain their dignity and to make sure their derby hats would not slip off.

A four-story building—owned by the meatpacking tycoon John Plankington—with small colonnades around each of the nine windows on its upper floors stood empty on the corner. Harris Brothers Fair, Wholesale Confectionery and Lager Beer Hall had occupied it at different times in the past. All three businesses had opened and closed at this location, and the site was considered to be unlucky. Across the street, a ramshackle collection of narrow, two-story buildings was covered with signs; it would be kind to call this block "over signed." The sign for Winkler's Cigar Headquarters and a sign touting the incredible value of "3 shots for 5 cents" indicated whose company the new Gimbels store would be keeping.

Jacob Gimbel knew his father was no stranger to taking risks. In May 1835, at the age of seventeen, Adam Gimbel had grown tired of toiling in the baron's vineyards near the village of Rhein-Pfaltz, Bavaria, and had worked as a ship's hand on a small square rigger to pay for his passage to New Orleans. He had already educated himself by learning Bible history from an itinerant rabbi, studied mathematics with a local Lutheran pastor and read books from the pastor's library. As an eighteen-year-old dock worker, Adam Gimbel worked the wharfs, unloading the cotton, vegetables, wheat and other commodities traveling down the Mississippi on large, wood-fired paddle boats and loading cargo into the waiting sailing ships tied up at the wharfs. Adam Gimbel was a keen observer, taking detailed notes on what commodities and finished goods were being shipped up and down the river. He noticed itinerant peddlers with huge, waterproof packs on their backs hiking north with the goods from New Orleans for resale. These peddlers served the isolated farms along the Mississippi Valley, bringing both merchandise and the news for their farming customers. The peddlers would be warmly greeted when they arrived at local farms to sell their goods.

In July 1837, after working the docks for two years, Adam Gimbel headed north at the age of twenty with his own pack of needles, thread and bolts of cloth on his back. His honesty and fairness—coupled with his habit of writing down people's special requests in the black book he carried with him—soon made him one of the favorite peddlers on the circuit. He printed handbills in New Orleans with lists of the items for sale and nailed them to trees on his route, an early version of target marketing. After almost five years as a peddler, he had built a solid business. He purchased a horse and wagon, allowing him to carry a wider assortment of goods on his route, and now he was able to stay at an inn when the weather was bad.

In 1842, Adam Gimbel arrived at Vincennes, Indiana, located just north of the point where the Wabash joined the Ohio River. According to *The Gimbel Family Tree* by Donald B. Gimbel in 1960, one theory of why Adam stopped in Vincennes was that he had "developed a serious case of diarrhea." Whatever the cause, the fact that Vincennes was located at the nexus of the well-traveled rivers of the Midwest gave him a good reason to stay. He rented a room in the Commercial House Hotel, set up a display of his merchandise and sold out his entire inventory in a week.

Excited by his success, he rented part of a house for his retail enterprise from Dr. Henry Fish, a local dentist. When Dr. Fish announced his retirement, Gimbel expanded his store to the entire house, calling it the "Palace of Trade." The series called *It All Began with Adam*—self-published by Gimbels Midwest in 1972–74 and used as promotional material—describes the store's inventory as "Nails, Gunpowder, Harnesses, Shawls, Shoes, Cloth, and Pelts" and proudly proclaimed, "Fairness and Equality to all patrons." Customers included Native Americans, who were often taken advantage of by unscrupulous traders and sold inferior goods in return for their valuable pelts. But Adam Gimbel gave the Native Americans the same impeccable treatment that he gave his other patrons, according to the promotional materials from Gimbels Midwest.

The two-and-a-half-story "Palace of Trade" housed a wide assortment of goods and offered customers the convenience of one-stop shopping. Instead of following the common practice of negotiating the selling price of items, Adam declared that his new store was the "One Price House." Adam also declared, "If anything done or said in this store looks wrong or is wrong, we would have our customers take it for granted that we shall set it right as soon as it comes to our knowledge. We are not satisfied unless our customers are."

His honesty was legendary. According to the lore of *It All Began with Adam*, Adam once followed a farmer for fifteen miles to give him the money from an overcharge on a cap. Another story written up in this promotional piece was of the Bishop of Vincennes riding up to Adam's store, tossing him a bag of gold and saying, "I haven't counted it. You count it and credit it to me, for when we both count you always find more than I. Besides, why should I bother to count money given to Adam Gimbel?" "A good name is better than riches" was Adam's motto. The country was in the midst of a depression when the store was started, but his bold merchandising principles carried him through difficult financial times.

Adam married Fridolyn Kahn-weiler in 1847, and they had fourteen children, eleven of whom lived to adulthood. It was this large family that supplied the merchandising talent that came to be known as Gimbel Brothers.

Standing on that street corner in 1886, Jacob Gimbel saw Milwaukee as a city, as John Gurda describes in *The Making of Milwaukee*, where hardworking people could find ready employment, buy a house, maybe raise a pig and send their children to school. Jacob recommended to his father, Adam, that they open a store at the corner of Wisconsin and Grand.

Attracted by the large German population in Milwaukee, the Gimbel family sold all their property in Vincennes and moved to Milwaukee in 1887, buying the "unlucky" store from John Plankington. The new store, with four stories, each thirty by one hundred feet in size, featured bright gaslights to make the broad range of merchandise more attractive. A large sign on top of the building, facing east, declared "carpets Gimbels dry goods." The same year, the seven Gimbel brothers—Jacob, Ellis, Isaac, Charles, Louis, Daniel and Benedict—purchased and opened a seven-story dry goods store in Philadelphia.

There were about two dozen retail dry goods stores in Milwaukee at that time. Each was small and carried a limited inventory, selling yard goods and sewing notions. Some merchants combined dry goods with groceries, hats or men's furnishings. A typical store might be twenty-two by sixty feet, a little more than 10 percent of the size of the new Gimbels store.

Milwaukee's downtown retail district developed unevenly over an eight-block area split by the river. Wisconsin Avenue west of the river, first known as Spring Street, was renamed Grand Avenue in 1876. The western leg of Wisconsin Avenue started at an area that was originally low marshland and was prone to flooding. Development had only started in 1846, and landfill had to be hauled in to get the level up high enough to install sewers for the buildings being planned. Wisconsin Avenue east of the river, with its higher

Gimbel's first store. *Courtesy of Bud Schneider.*

elevation, was much easier to develop as a commercial area. The spread-out downtown commercial district made it easier for neighborhoods such as Third Street and Vliet Street to develop their own retail centers.

The Gimbels store had a single elevator for the four floors, a delivery person, a window trimmer, three office people and forty to seventy-five salespeople. In addition to a gents' furnishing department, the first floor offered a rainbow of colorful dress goods in silks, velvets, flannels and muslin, along with all the laces, ribbons and buttons that were needed to complete the new dresses. The cloak department was on the second floor. The third and fourth floors featured a big selection of carpets, rugs, curtains and tapestries. The store also featured a year-round toy department and sold sheet music and pianos. Music was constantly playing on a phonograph in that department for the shoppers' entertainment.

The Gimbels store was staffed mostly by women who started their 8:00 a.m. to 6:00 p.m. shifts by calling their number to the time keeper at the employee entrance, six days a week. The store was not open on Sundays, but often employees had to come in to restock the shelves. Female employees usually brought their lunch and ate it in the women's restroom in the basement of the store. Salaries ranged from $1.50 to $7.00 per week.

There were no child labor laws, and child labor was quite common in 1894. Hilda Satt Polacheck writes in her autobiography, *I Came as a Stranger: The Story of a Hull House Girl*, that one in every five children was working long hours every day by the age of thirteen or fourteen.

In addition to the cash girls, transfer girls and boys would take merchandise to the central bundling desk, where the customers picked up their purchases before leaving the store. Later, a mechanized system of overhead wire baskets carried money between the clerks in the departments and the transfer desk on the balcony, according to the records at the Milwaukee County Historical Society.

Gimbels on Grand Avenue offered easy credit terms, free delivery and promoted its sales in both the English and German newspapers. Customers lined up at the door every Friday for Bargain Days. The delivery fleet consisted of a stable of forty horses and twenty-four drivers, each of whom had a horse boy to help. Every credit transaction had to be authorized by the credit department located at the transfer desk, and if a salesperson failed to follow this procedure and the customer did not pay, the salesperson had the purchase deducted from her check. The lay-away and COD departments offered methods for customers to make purchases if they were not credit worthy.

Adam Gimbel died in 1896 at the age of seventy-nine. Louis Gimbel managed the Milwaukee store from 1894 to 1910, while Isaac became the head of the entire firm. The large family that Adam and Fridolyn started became a strong bench of management talent, enabling the company to expand rapidly. The five Gimbel sons who married had eight sons of their own, all of whom were involved in the company at some point.

SCHUSTER'S

Gimbels had one important competitor in Milwaukee: Schuster's. In 1883, four years before Adam Gimbel opened his four-story department store in downtown Milwaukee, Ed Schuster had purchased half ownership of a modest dry goods store at Twelfth and Walnut from Jacob Poss. Renaming the store Poss & Schuster, the fifty-two-year-old Schuster looked forward to settling down. Born in Driburg, Westphalia, Germany, he had traveled to Australia, back to Germany and then to the United States looking for his fortune. He, too, was attracted to Milwaukee because of its large German community, which at that time, according to John Gurda in *The Making of Milwaukee*, made up 27 percent of the city's population.

A year later, in 1884, Edward Schuster was doing well enough to open his own store at 2107 North Third Street, taking his nineteen-year-old clerk, Albert T. Friedman, into the business with him. Edward opened his store in the center of a thriving Milwaukee neighborhood. Burleigh Street, eleven blocks north, was Milwaukee's northern boundary, and Thirty-fifth Street was its western boundary, with houses built up to Twenty-seventh Street. Wooden sidewalks lined Third Street, a road that was so deep in mud in wet weather that oxen teams hauling loads of cedar got mired. Getting around was easy; it cost five cents to take a single-horse streetcar.

Edward Schuster's merchandising strategy was to focus on those neighborhood locations, and he eschewed a site in the central business district. He was known for his good sense of humor and the courtesy he extended to his customers. He offered friendly service and good values to his community and delivered customer purchases by streetcar or bicycle. Free parking for his customers' bicycles and baby carriages was readily available and became one of Schuster's store's signatures as it expanded.

Schuster's first store. *Courtesy of Bud Schneider.*

The stores were open long hours, from 7:30 a.m. to 9:00 p.m. Monday through Friday, with a late closing of 10:00 p.m. on Saturdays and opening Sunday mornings, 8:00 a.m. to noon. Merchandise was displayed on the sidewalk in front of the store, and if a rainstorm threatened, the clerks hustled to get the items into the store before they got wet.

Schuster used eleven- by fourteen-inch flyers in both English and German to advertise his stores. In 1887, he started distributing a free weekly newspaper called the *Schuster's Weekly*, filled with advertising and tips for living. Barefoot boys were paid thirty-five cents to distribute the weekly.

In 1888, Ed Schuster expanded his store at Third and Brown and again expanded the store a year later. In 1893, the store was destroyed by fire, and a new store was built at the same location. In 1894, a second Schuster store opened at Twelfth and Walnut Streets, adjacent to the location where Ed Schuster had been a partner in his first venture. Working conditions were similar to those found at Gimbels, with employees ringing the time bell when they checked in and walking home for lunch, with a one-hour to ninety-minute lunch hour. Pay was two dollars per week, but you could have a half-day's pay docked from your check if you were thirty minutes late.

THE ECONOMY

The Panic of 1893 started with credit drying up and rapidly expanded to many banks and manufacturers. Banks and companies closed or, at best, laid off workers. The depression lasted until 1897, but it was not until 1898 that business turned around.

As Gurda writes, the economy roared back to life in 1898, and the city's machine shops were shipping three times more products in 1890 than they had ten years earlier. The foundries and rolling mills were producing iron and steel for manufacturing industries throughout the entire country. Other local manufacturing plants were making electric motors, gasoline engines and steam turbines to power the nation.

The nine local breweries, aided by aggressive national advertising campaigns, were shipping more beer annually than those of either New York or St. Louis. The city, because of its large supply of hemlock trees, was the dominant producer of tanned hides for the eastern seaboard's shoe factories.

John Plankington and Patrick Cudahy took the business of butchering hogs to a new level, selling their products nationally and even to the British navy. Creative manufacturers made sausage from the meat scraps, turned fat into lard and made glue out of pigs' feet, brushes out of their bristles and fertilizer out of their blood and bones. The rapid growth of these industries, with their large payrolls, made Milwaukee a good place for retail. Family-sustaining jobs were plentiful, and people had money to spend.

As the nineteenth century ended, Milwaukee had two dominant retail institutions: Gimbels, which offered selection, competitive pricing and a downtown location, and Schuster's, which offered two convenient neighborhood locations with friendly customer service. The city's economic engine was running on all cylinders, people had jobs and both stores were thriving.

TIMELINE

1817	Adam Gimbel is born in Bavarian highlands, village of Rhein-Pfaltz
1831	Edward Schuster is born in Westphalia
May 1835	Adam Gimbel arrives in New Orleans
July 1837	Adam Gimbel begins his career as an itinerant peddler
1842	Adam Gimbel opens store in Vincennes
1883	Edward Schuster migrates to United States
1883	Edward Schuster opens his store at Twelfth and Walnut
1884	Ed Schuster and Albert Friedman open a store on Third Street

Milwaukee's Beloved Department Stores

April 10, 1885	Adam Gimbel's son, Bernard Gimbel, is born in Vincennes, Indiana
1886	Jacob Gimbel finds the site for the Milwaukee store
1887	Adam Gimbel opens the Milwaukee store
1888	Ed Schuster moves into a larger store at Third and Brown Street
1889	Ed Schuster builds a new store at Third and Brown
1893	Fire destroys the Schuster's store at Third and Brown
1894	Ed Schuster opens a second store at Twelfth and Walnut
1894	Gimbel Brothers opens a store in Philadelphia
1894	Louis Gimbel takes over the Milwaukee store
1895	Ed Schuster reopens store at Third and Brown
1896	Adam Gimbel dies

CHAPTER 2

The Boom Years

1900–1920

G imbels dropped the apostrophe in its name around 1902, and the same year, it opened a new white terra cotta eight-story building with nine selling floors on what is now the corner of Plankington and Wisconsin. Gimbels also extended its footprint south by purchasing the low two-story buildings adjacent to its two main buildings on Wisconsin Avenue. A four-story building was completed in 1915 on the site of an outdoor produce market and a burlesque theater on the corner of what is now Michigan and Plankington.

The rambling buildings were connected with a maze of passages, rooftop boardwalks and outside stairs so their employees could save time and not be forced to walk all the way down to the first floor and then back up another staircase. The Gimbels store had 1,200 windows that were opened on warm summer days to bring in the westerly winds and cool the store. The Gimbels Grill Room was large enough that it could seat three hundred people for a private banquet. In 1916, the Plankington Hotel, a favorite of the Gimbel family, was torn down and replaced by the Plankington Mall.

Gimbels' two locations, in Milwaukee and Philadelphia, gave the company the volume needed to open its own European buying offices in 1903. This created a lot of excitement among the employees. According to a self-published brochure by Gimbels Midwest, *It All Began with Adam* (1972), the Gimbels Band met the yard goods and domestic buyer at the train station when he was returning from one of his early buying trips in Europe.

Gimbels around 1900. The apostrophe in the name was dropped in 1902. *Courtesy of Historic Photo Collection/Milwaukee Public Library.*

Business was good. Silk waistbands and matching bonnets, designed and made in the store, were bestsellers for the 1902 Easter season. A December 1904 Gimbels advertisement said that it was "growing and improving...for their customers" and was "a profitable business." Arthur Crofoot, the men's clothing buyer, came up with the idea of including a second pair of pants with the purchase of each suit, extending the suit's life for the customer.

In the later 1900s, Gimbels expanded under the leadership of an assortment of Adam Gimbel's offspring. In 1907, Adam's grandson Bernard Gimbel opened the Manhattan store, and Bernard's uncle Isaac Gimbel moved to New York to oversee the three stores of the family corporation. Oscar Greenwald, Adam Gimbel's oldest grandson, became store manager of the Milwaukee store in 1910, a position he held until his death in 1941.

Schuster's was growing too, adding selling area and new lines of merchandise. In 1900, the department store moved its Twelfth Street store to Eleventh Street and expanded it. A brand-new store was built at Third and Garfield in 1908. Schuster's started an upscale silk department in 1912, launching it with promotions of special purchases. The Victor-Victrola department opened the same year featuring Victrolas priced from fifteen dollars and up. The candy department and the Soda Fountain and Public Grill were added to the Third Street store in 1908. Schuster's built a new Twelfth Street store in 1911, and the Mitchell Street store opened in a neighborhood called the South Side Market, according to the *Milwaukee Journal*, in 1914. The Third Street store was doubled in size that same year and was called the "Colossus of Upper Third Street." Furniture, pianos and the ladies' beauty parlor were added to all three stores. In 1918, two additional floors were added to Schuster's Third Street store. The three stores now had 559 employees.

They added technology also. At Schuster's Third Street store, the first telephone system consisted of a single telephone and a buzzer system for the people in the head office. In 1901, the company installed a materials-handling system that moved deliveries from the bundling desk to the basement with a water-powered elevator. Messenger boys riding motorized bicycles carried large sacks tossed over their shoulders to make deliveries, and teams of mules pulled wagons on the longer routes. The first autos were

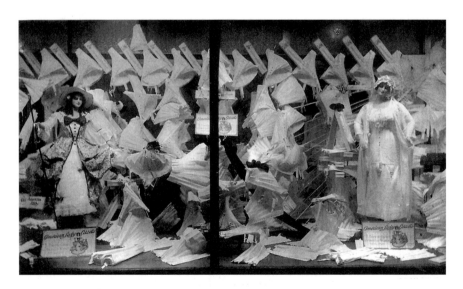

The window of American Lady Corsets at Schuster's. *Courtesy of Milwaukee County Historical Society.*

used for deliveries in 1912, and by 1914, Kisels and Menominee trucks were delivering packages to Schuster's customers.

Display windows mirrored the differing personalities of the two department stores. Gimbels' windows were themed and focused, reflecting influences from its Manhattan store. Schuster's windows were less sophisticated and featured highly visible price tags on the wide-ranging display of items carried in the store. Schuster's advertised every week ten to fifteen special purchases with its hand-delivered flyer, the *Schuster's Weekly*. A 1915 employee newsletter boasted that "the boom is here...the wheat crop was excellent, and factories are taxed to their maximum."

EMPLOYEE TRAINING

Gimbels and Schuster's offered untrained workers a way to participate in the booming economy. Both businesses put considerable resources into training their employees so that they would be pleasant and helpful salespeople. The dress code for women was black dresses made out of silk, satin or crepe, and men wore sleeve protectors, vests and ties, even during the summer months. The stores were cold in the winter, but wearing a sweater for comfort was against the dress code. Gimbels waitresses wore large white bows in their hair, knee-length white aprons and long black dresses. Working as a sales clerk on the selling floor or in the display department was a stable, family-sustaining job, and employees stayed. A 1962 full-page Gimbels ad featured 30 associates who were joining the twenty-five-year club with its 554 members; in addition, 13 associates were joining the fifty-year club, and 2 were being inducted into the sixty-year club. Other newspaper clippings from that time noted that corsages were given to Mrs. Elizabeth Amidon, who had worked at Gimbels for fifty years, and Miss Frances Mareth, who was a marking supervisor and had completed sixty-three years. In 1965, Ed Danaher had completed sixty years of service. He started as a transfer boy at the age of sixteen in 1905, and at the age of seventy-six, he was the main aisle manager in the Milwaukee store.

Keeping in Touch (K.I.T.) was a monthly employee publication produced by Schuster's that promoted ways for employees to improve their sales. They were asked to study grammar after hours, to obey and told to "get out or get in line." Tact, described as "knowing how to pull the stinger out of the bee without being stung," was encouraged.

Albert Friedman, the general manager of Schuster's after Ed Schuster died in 1904, wrote in his pamphlet titled *The Story of Annie Smith* about the career of seventeen-year-old Annie, who was "a picture of health, good natured and we might even say, attractive." Annie started in the housewares department and was promoted based on her performance to the cloak department with better sales and commissions potential. Annie was good at the soft sell and encouraging customers to shop the store's advertised specials. Suggestion selling was encouraged through a hypothetical purchase in *The Story of Annie Smith*: "He [the customer] bought in addition a sample of a new make of fruit jar costing four times as much as the ordinary kind simply because he had been convinced by the able saleswoman that this jar was more practical."

Schuster's gave its salespeople monthly reports on their individual sales and paid bonuses every February 1 based on sales performance. Burroughs adding machines were used in the laborious task of tabulating every handwritten sales check to determine each individual's sales totals.

Working behind the counter at Schuster's was a job where an unmarried young person could be recognized for her abilities and her willingness to work. It was considered to be a genteel prelude to getting married and raising a family.

Customer satisfaction was the goal, as stated on the back of a Schuster's 1913 sales check: "We do not consider this transaction closed until YOU ARE SATISFIED. It is on this basis only that we solicit your patronage. ED. SCHUSTER & Co., Inc." Schuster's offered one dollar for any errors customers found in its advertisements.

The delivery department sent a horse-drawn sleigh to deliver two dozen comforters ordered by a group of people holed up in a hotel after a big snowstorm, according to a 1953 issue of *Keeping in Touch*. It took an entire day to deliver the merchandise and then make the journey back to the store's barn.

EMPLOYEE MORALE

Both companies hosted annual picnics for their employees at Waukesha Beach amusement park, providing special trains to take employees out and back. For a few years, Oscar Greenwald, the Gimbels store manager, moved the picnic to his one-hundred-acre estate, Pine Woods, located near the border of New Berlin. Employees were asked to bring their own box lunches and were treated to soda and ice cream and given tours of the barns and grounds. After a year or two, Greenwald moved the annual picnic back to Waukesha Beach, complaining that the crowd made too great of a mess on his estate.

The three-store Schuster's annual picnic was more magnanimous, with the company providing a picnic lunch and a whole day of special events. Activities included five-inning baseball games, a fifty-yard dash for fat men (175 pounds or more), a needle-threading contest for men, a tug of war and greased pole walking. Peanut and potato races were provided for the women and children. Women attended in long dresses, and men wore coats, vests, ties and derby hats. According to picnic planning notes from 1916, the Schuster's store song was sung to the music of "On Wisconsin." The first verse was "Always Schuster's, ever Schuster's, Schuster's is our goal. For we all are Schuster boosters, Clear from head to toe."

Schuster's *Keeping in Touch* described its first employee minstrel show at Plankington Hall in December 1912. Minstrel shows were a precursor to vaudeville and were popular at the time for combining song, dance and humor. Although considered stereotyping and unenlightened today, these shows were not necessarily meant to denigrate African Americans. Rather, minstrel shows were seen as a window into the culture of the approximately two thousand African Americans who had migrated from the South and were living in Milwaukee in the early 1900s. Employees, some wearing black face, provided stand-up humor, dancing and choral selections. By 1920, the annual minstrel show, with a greatly expanded budget of almost $19,000 (in today's dollars), was moved to the Pabst Theater. This expanded production featured an interlocutor, or a master of ceremonies, who was the straight man for the fast-talking comedians in black face, called "ends" or "end men." The provocative female named Topsie; a seventy-voice choir that performed nine selections, including "High Old Time in Dixie"; and dancers completed the cast. The program ended with a musical finale of songs from around the world. The amateur chorus members were dressed up in national garb from such exotic locations as Venice, Spain and Hawaii. Working at Schuster's was not dull.

Schuster's three-store picnics, inter-store baseball games, dances, minstrel show and men's, girls' and boys' bands were used to build employee morale and create a bond between management and employees. Store meetings, which sometimes included training, were used to make Schuster's employees feel that they were an important part of the company. *Keeping in Touch* from 1912 exhorts employees to work twice as hard for Schuster's success.

Gimbels employees loved to socialize on their own, including boarding a boat named *Bloomer Girl* docked on the river and motoring up the lakeshore to Whitefish Bay, where they would party. Another favorite spot to meet was the Schlitz Palm Garden. Department socials and masquerade parties were held in Gimbels employees' homes. Staff on each selling floor would put on plays before store opening.

WORLD WAR I

Times were good: 38 percent of Milwaukeeans were homeowners, Henry Ford was paying his workers one dollar a day and, although the stock market was in a slump, demand was high for Milwaukee products because of the start of World War I.

During the war, patriotic rallies of Gimbels employees were held on the street-level floor in the morning before store opening. "It's a Long Way to Tipperary" was everyone's favorite song. Gift boxes were sent to Gimbels employees in the service. Parties for wounded servicemen were held in the Ravenswood Hospital, with employees bringing gift boxes supplied by Gimbels for the recovering servicemen. Many men from Schuster's also served in the army, and their letters were published in the monthly employee publications. Employees sold thrift stamps for the war effort and manned the store float in the Liberty Bond Procession, and the Schuster's men's band marched in the Preparedness Parade. On Armistice Day, November 11, 1918, people sang in the elevators and danced on Grand Avenue. Schuster's closed, and its employees paraded down Wisconsin Avenue in celebration.

World War I created a strong demand for Milwaukee's pork, leather, motorcycles and machine parts; companies needed workers. Women were now working in the factories that competed for labor with the department stores. Many Milwaukee companies hosted summer picnics and holiday parties as ways to keep their employees happy and discourage unions. Milwaukee's voters installed two Socialist mayors, Emil Seidel in 1910 and

Daniel Hoan in 1916, and their philosophy of treating employees as valuable resources became more accepted. Women's suffrage became law in August 1920, and women started to have a voice at the polls.

Gimbels had separate management teams in its stores in Milwaukee, Philadelphia and New York, but the three teams would share information about bestsellers. The Gimbels New York store provided a window to East Coast trends and enabled the Gimbels Milwaukee store to be in the forefront of these new trends.

In spite of the fact that Prohibition, which took effect in June 1919, took Milwaukee's large brewing industries off the map, Milwaukee's economy was strong, and both Gimbels and Schuster's were poised to take advantage of it. According to Gurda, Milwaukee's manufacturing output increased by 158 percent from 1914 to 1919, and 58 percent of Milwaukee's labor force in 1920 was working in manufacturing. This growth had created very dense living conditions, which at first played to Schuster's strength with its neighborhood stores. It became more difficult for Schuster's to compete with Gimbels in the long run, however, as people started moving to the suburbs.

TIMELINE

1902	Gimbels opens its new store at the corner of Wisconsin and Plankington
1908	Schuster's builds a new store on Third Street
May 3, 1909	Bernard Gimbel supervises construction of Manhattan store
September 29, 1910	Louis Gimbel resigns as store manager of the Milwaukee store and takes over management of the Manhattan store
1910	Oscar Greenwald becomes the store manager of Gimbels

1911	Schuster's builds a new store at Twelfth and Vliet
1914	Schuster's opens its Mitchell Street store
1914	Schuster's doubles the size of its Third Street store
1918	Schuster's adds two floors to its Third Street store
1919–20	Gimbels expands with both a four-floor and seven-floor building

Chapter 3

From Boom to Bust

1920–1930

Famous Gimbels Promotions

Business was good after World War I, and Gimbels expanded its merchandise offerings with specialty items and enhanced the store's decor. The groceries and delicatessen department on the fifth floor ground coffee to order and displayed a wide variety of spices and teas in bulk containers. The ornate arches of the main floor were lined with decorative lights to give this key shopping area more sparkle.

Friday Bargain Days were replaced by major sales event like Gimbels Days, Founder's Days, Daring Days and the Anniversary Sale. In the early 1920s, Gimbels put on a Thanksgiving Day parade, dressing employees up in costumes and putting them on floats that started at Gesu Church and finished at Gimbels. During the Christmas holidays, Gimbels employees would dress up in costumes such as the Wild Man from Borneo and parade through the store, teasing the children they encountered. The employees all pitched in to help promote the store. For example, the mattress salesperson reclined in a double bed on the selling floor with an overweight man next to him for an entire week to prove that the mattress would not sag.

Gimbels experimented with its own radio station, WAAK, housed in a small, airless and very warm room on the third floor. As amateur musicians performed, people would call in on the telephone, and the announcer would repeat their comments over the air. Crystal radios were built out of Quaker Oats boxes and placed, with headsets, throughout the store. Customers were encouraged to come into the store and listen to amateur performances during the limited broadcast hours. People living out as far as Thirty-fifth Street were amazed when they found they could pick up the radio signals from this groundbreaking broadcast studio. Holeproof Hosiery Company purchased the station's first radio spot. The radio station broadcast intermittently for three years, from 1922 to 1925.

Gimbels promoted its ability to purchase distressed goods from bankrupt stores and offer them at close-out prices in the Economy Basement Store that opened in 1926. Hourly specials were announced with the striking of a big gong. The Economy Basement Store even featured its own soda fountain where ham and roast beef sandwiches were sold. Gimbels purchased the entire stock of Oriental and antique rugs from the Philadelphia Sesquicentennial and hung them on every rack available on the main aisle of the first floor of the Milwaukee store. This inelegant display sold a lot of rugs.

The Gimbels Nemo Corset Semi Annual Sale was one of epic proportions. Eighty-five salespeople were required to staff it, and fitting rooms were spread around using sheets hung on iron pipes. There was a sense of danger that the sheets would slide off the metal pipes and expose the women trying on corsets, as this had occurred at least once. The corsets were priced at $1.98, $2.98 and $3.50, and entire counters filled with merchandise were sold off before noon on the first day of the sale.

Horace Saks and Bernard Gimbel were friends; they traveled with each other and enjoyed an occasional competitive round of golf. In 1923, on a return train trip from Jersey Shores, Bernard and Horace reached an agreement for Gimbels to buy Saks for 8.1 million shares of Gimbels stock. This was the origin of the annual Saks 5th Avenue seasonal merchandise sale in the Economy Basement Store.

"MEET ME DOWN BY SCHUSTER'S, WHERE THE STREETCAR BENDS THE CORNER"

Schuster's continued to promote in its own unique, creative way. Its sixteenth annual voting contest was kicked off at the end of August 1922. This was a promotion where shoppers were given postcards and the salesperson checked off one vote, or box, with every fifty-cent purchase. These cards were cashed in at the end of January, with cash rewards given to both the shopper and the charity of the shopper's choice.

Customers were also given Schuster's Stamps with every purchase, and they were also given out at grocery, hardware and jewelry stores and gas stations—170 to 300 local stores in all. Stamps offered customers additional savings and promoted customer loyalty. Directions for use of the stamp books were printed in English, German and Polish on the inside covers. A stamp book filled with two thousand stamps, all carefully licked and mounted, could be redeemed at Schuster's for one dollar. Customers received different numbers of stamps with their purchases, ranging from two stamps to five, for every ten-cent purchase increment. Customers received 1 to 2 percent cash back on their purchases, receiving the lower rate on the popular shopping days of Monday, Friday and Saturday and the higher rate on the slower shopping days of Tuesday, Wednesday and Thursday.

The *Schuster's Weekly*, a six- or eight-page newspaper-sized flyer, advertised a new sale every Monday. Schuster's merchants had thirteen days' lead time to submit items to the advertising department, and the advertising manager determined which items would be featured. Artists created the illustrations from samples submitted by the buyers. Every week, 115,000 to 250,000 copies of the flyer were dropped off at delivery stations, where Schuster's scouts hand delivered them to almost every home in Milwaukee and thirty-six suburbs.

The Schuster's merchandising approach was not always the most elegant. A 1925 manuscript describes the display window at the Twelfth street store as "three windows with a curtain rod, from which they draped everything they sold, hosiery, ribbons, embroidery, corsets and notions, in the most beautiful merchandise hash." The window trimmer was pretty handy with electrical gadgets because he was also the maintenance man. One window trimmer invented an instrument made out of an alarm clock, housed it in a cigar box and used it to turn the lights of the windows on and off.

GROWTH

Marcella Haerter, a longtime salesperson, tells about a tunnel that was used to move Gimbels' merchandise from stockrooms in the buildings on Michigan and Plankington to the Grand Avenue selling floor. It replaced the alley that originally ran north–south in the center of the block between the buildings and the river. Gimbels made its first public stock offering in 1922, funding the construction of two buildings and filling in the gap between the structures on Wisconsin Avenue and Michigan Street. Construction started in 1923, and the buildings were completed in 1925. Now there were eight floors stretching between the anchor buildings on Wisconsin Avenue and Michigan Street.

A construction platform was extended into the Milwaukee River, with this platform becoming one of the first segments of today's City of Milwaukee RiverWalk. Over the years, the idea of using the platform over the river as an outside dining area for a restaurant was proposed, but the high winds and the annual alewives' migration up the river caused problems. Pranksters throwing tables and chairs into the river added to the expense.

The majestic ornate columns on the block-long Gimbels façade facing the river emulated columns on the façade of Selfridge's Department Store in London. A nine-foot-wide shopping arcade facing Wisconsin Avenue, with three entrances, was the main feature on the first floor of the Gimbels building. In 1925, five stories were added onto the neighboring Plankington Arcade.

Schuster's enlarged its Mitchell Street Store in 1921 and expanded its Twelfth Street store in 1924. By 1926, it had 2,300 employees and its own New York buying office. The company saw itself as marching to its own drummer, neither sharing its strategies with any other retail organization nor doing any joint purchasing. It felt it had a competitive edge over Gimbels, which had opened its fourth store in Pittsburgh in 1926. There were other competitors, such as Sears and Roebuck's at Twenty-seventh and North and both the Boston Store and T.A. Chapman's on Wisconsin Avenue. Most of the city was electrified by then, stimulating a rush on electric appliance departments opening in every store.

BILLIE THE BROWNIE

At 7:30 p.m. on November 26, 1927, several years after Gimbels ended its Thanksgiving parade, Schuster's had its first Christmas parade. Two streetcar platforms, pulled by a streetcar tender, carried Santa and his reindeer. Me-Tik, the Eskimo reindeer handler, and Billie the Brownie, Santa's special helper and advance man, rode along. These characters were joined by Cinderella, the Three Pigs, the Big Bad Wolf, Peter Rabbit, Peter the Pumpkin Eater and the Cow that Jumped Over the Moon. The festive group traveled in grand style, lighted by a galaxy of sparkling battery-powered electric lights, with the mood enhanced by the amplified sound of "Jingle Bells." They traversed south down the lakefront on what is now Lincoln Memorial Drive, turned west on Wisconsin Avenue past Gimbels and ended the glorious parade at Eleventh Street.

This was a truly magical event for the city's children and their parents, who turned out in numbers never seen before in Milwaukee. Children who had their doubts about Santa now believed when they saw his live reindeer. The city used 75 policemen to manage the estimated crowd of 100,000 parade watchers. This was a crowd that was larger, said the *Milwaukee Journal*, than the one that had come to see Charles Lindbergh earlier that year when he visited Milwaukee after flying across the Atlantic.

Schuster's had mounted a teaser advertising campaign with daily bulletins starting two weeks before the Thanksgiving parade. Santa sent telegrams asking Schuster's to prepare Toyland for him and describing the long, arduous trip from the North Pole that Santa, his reindeer, Me-Tik and Billie the Brownie were on. The telegrams from Santa Claus were posted in the windows of the Western Union office on Wisconsin Avenue. Billie the Brownie also issued his own reports, such as "Live reindeer coming, a thrill in store for all Milwaukee; Boys & Girls…ringing with excitement."

Billie the Brownie kept the children's attention with:

> *Boys and girls—listen! Far from the north comes the distant sound of prancing feet. The mighty polar bear stops in his tracks to listen. In-You-Gee-To, the great Eskimo hunter, pauses in his chase after the Arctic wolf, ravenous dog teams yowl and the Auk soars swiftly across the plains of ice and snow. Something unusual! Shall we tell you what it is?*
>
> *Well you might know now. Santa Claus is driving his reindeer to Milwaukee. Yes, sir—live reindeer pounding down from the north headed straight for Milwaukee—that's the thrill in store for you. Santa is on his way to Milwaukee! Steeds of the north wind, the reindeer, bear him swiftly onward.*

All of this came from Schuster's advertising department. The idea for Billie the Brownie came from a 1900 book by Palmer Cox about brownies. A graphic artist created the image, and the copywriters came up with the daily messages. They timed Santa's arrival in Milwaukee, an event talked about by the entire town, to be just on the cusp of the Christmas selling season.

The following year, Schuster's used a new advertising tool to build on the wild success of its first Thanksgiving parade—radio. WTMJ, which was owned by the *Milwaukee Journal*, ran a children's radio program called the *Seckatary* (secretary misspelled) *Hawkins Radio Club* weekdays from 5:30 p.m. to 6:00 p.m. and for an entire hour on Sundays. This was a takeoff of a syndicated column that ran in many papers nationally, including the *Milwaukee Journal*. Hawkins was the imaginary young man who could not spell but was secretary of the club. On November 18, 1928, the announcer, Larry Teich, announced Santa's arrival in Milwaukee and invited everyone to the upcoming Schuster's Christmas parade. Schuster's advertising department had sketched creative plans for the three flat streetcars that would bear the floats. Almost fifty men were toiling away in Schuster's Cold Spring shops creating these floats, with no expense being spared.

Santa's trip from the North Pole had been even longer and more dangerous than that of the previous year. Some of the reindeer got seasick in the rough waters on the stormy sea off the West Coast, and the hardy group encountered a fearsome blizzard while crossing the Rockies. All of

Boys and girls at Tippecanoe School, Cudahy, with Santa, Me-Tik and reindeer in the background, December 15, 1927. *Courtesy of Milwaukee County Historical Society.*

these adventures were reported in great detail on the radio as Santa made his journey. Teich read letters over the air from the children in the listening audience, and additional letters were printed in Schuster's Christmas newsletter, *Reindeer News*.

Crowds gathered at Thirty-eighth and McKinley in 1928 to observe the exit from the staging area of the three railcars and the tug as it pulled out into the parade route. The lighted floats became even more magical because of a lake effect snowstorm that struck in the evening. The crowds were even larger than the previous year, with one hundred policemen needed for crowd control. The officers tried to keep the children from cutting the lines and approaching Santa. One officer said, as reported by Ralph Luedtke in his history of Billie the Brownie, "Whatter you going to do? You can't get hard with them youngsters when they get such a kick out of it." Eight missing boys were located at the Christmas parade by the police, and two boys were found waiting at Schuster's front door the following day at 5:00 a.m. to see Santa. After the parade, Santa, Me-Tik (whose real name was Alex) and the reindeer set up shop at the stables of Schuster's Twelfth Street store.

BLACK FRIDAY

October 24, 1929 (Black Thursday), and the following day, called Black Friday, brought the stock market crash and, with it, the Depression. Gurda writes about how business and political leaders such as Herman Falk, the CEO of First Wisconsin, and Mayor Daniel Hoan talked bravely about how Milwaukee's economy would weather the storm. President Hoover told the country, "The fundamental business of the country…is on a sound and prosperous basis." They were wrong. Milwaukee started seeing substantial unemployment the very next year.

The period of Gimbels' and Schuster's rapid expansion had ended, with the exception of Schuster's completing its Commerce Street warehouse in 1930. This building housed its service operations, including the delivery, warehouse bundling, receiving and marking. In addition to housing reserve stockrooms and the fur vault, the workrooms for carpet, draperies, shades, furniture, radio, Servel gas refrigerators and major appliance departments were in this new building. The Commerce Street fur vault had a small anteroom with a phone so the workers could get used to the chill and be able

Gimbels Commerce Street Warehouse in the 1970s. *Courtesy of Jack Koplin.*

Gimbels Commerce Street today. *Courtesy of Paul Geenen.*

to call if they got locked in. The vault itself had cork walls and galvanized racks to store five thousand coats.

A period that later came to be called the Roaring Twenties, with everyone working, factories humming and shipping products all over the world, ended with a Depression that was unimaginable in its depths. Both Gimbels and Schuster's had gone on a building binge that came to a crashing end. Selling costs, the wages paid to the salespeople, was the single largest expense in these department stores, and they began to trim sales staff and find the optimal balance between customer service and profitability.

TIMELINE

1921	Schuster's expands the Mitchell Street store
April 26, 1922	Gimbels starts an experimental radio station
1922	Gimbel Brothers makes its first stock offering
1923	Gimbels builds an eight-story building next to Wisconsin and the Milwaukee River
1923	Horace Saks and Bernard Gimbel agree to Gimbel Brothers' purchase of Saks
1924	Schuster's expands its Twelfth Street store
1925	Gimbel Brothers purchases Kaufmann & Baer Department Store in Pittsburgh and changes the name to Gimbels
1925	Gimbels adds a new building with eight floors
1926	Gimbels opens its Economy Basement Store
November 26, 1927	Schuster's first Christmas parade begins

November 18, 1928	WTMJ mentions Billie the Brownie for the first time
1929	Bernard Gimbel hires Charles Zadok to manage Gimbels' European buying offices

CHAPTER 4

The Depression

1930–1940

BROTHER, CAN YOU SPARE A DIME?

Company mergers before the start of the Depression had made it very difficult for small companies to get the financial resources they needed, and they closed at an alarming rate in the early 1930s. Large companies had to take drastic steps to survive but managed to limp through this difficult financial period.

In 1929, Bernard Gimbel hired Charles Zadok to lead Gimbels' European buying offices. Zadok, born in Salonik, Greece, in 1896, had completed his education in Paris and London. In 1936, Gimbels brought Zadok to the United States and appointed him vice-president and general manager of the Gimbels Milwaukee store, while Oscar Greenwald continued to hold his office of president.

In 1930, Congress passed the Hawley-Smoot Tariff, raising the cost of over twenty thousand imported goods to protect American agricultural and industrial jobs. Affected countries imposed their own retaliatory tariffs on goods made in America. Milwaukee, with its heavy manufacturing base, suffered even greater unemployment than the rest of the country. In 1933, according to Gurda, 53 percent of the property taxes owed the city went uncollected, and wages had dropped by 64.5 percent. Unemployment worsened, with 25 percent of workers unemployed by 1933. National income dropped by 54 percent, according to Stanley Schultz in *The Great Depression: A Primary Source for History*. In 1933, the Gimbels credit manager,

August C. Wehl, led the development of a program run by the Association of Commerce that negotiated payment plans for people over their heads in debt. Gimbels' heavy reliance on sales and special purchases, *Schuster's Weekly* sale flyers and both companies' use of part-time help carried the two department stores through the difficult financial times of the 1930s.

GIMBELS UPDATES MAIN FLOOR

Zadok updated the main floor of the Gimbels Milwaukee store by removing the ornate arches whose edges were lined with not-too-subtle lights and installing a soda fountain near the Plankington Street door. The delicatessen and grocery departments replaced the piece goods department, which was moved upstairs. Escalators and bright florescent lighting were installed, and two restaurants were added, the first-floor Tasty Town restaurant and a more formal restaurant called the Eighth Floor Restaurant.

Bernard Gimbel was one of the sponsors of the New York World's Fair and worked with people from the Westinghouse Company in planning the fair. When the fair closed, Gimbel purchased two escalators from the fair for the Gimbels Milwaukee store. There was much fanfare when the first two escalators were installed. People lined up to take a ride to the second floor. It seemed like such a good idea that Gimbel purchased six more. These escalators were unusual in that they were thirty-six inches in width and the slotted steps were composed of a black material called micarta. The serial numbers of these escalators were one through eight. Since the escalators were not built to fit the Gimbels building, each floor had to be modified to accommodate the new equipment, resulting in the floors being wavy and uneven.

Over the years, Tasty Town became known as a popular gathering place for interesting people of all stripes, according to columnist Bill Janz. Lois Schmidt, who worked at Gimbels as a part-time flyer during the 1930s, later recalled that she could "still taste those chocolate phosphate they served at the Tasty Town counters." Schmidt's job as a "flyer" meant that she covered for regular employees while they took their breaks, and she also helped out if a department got busy. Two of her favorite departments were the toy department and the infant department, where salespeople in white uniforms with starched caps advised customers. She recalls that in the '30s, the uniformed "Elevator Girls," as the Gimbels *Broadcaster* called them, always wore spotless white gloves. At 3:00 p.m. daily, Schmidt was charged with walking through the entire store, from the basement to the sixth floor, to count customers. Then she would walk to the Boston Store to do the same there.

Gimbels continued to use a highly promotional marketing approach, with the Economy Basement Store leading the way. Schmidt recalls the difficult financial times of the Depression and the "wonderful purchases in the basement." The spring rains that flooded the Basement Store every year created some damp bargains. In 1932, "Gimbels New Deal Jubilee Sale" celebrated Franklin Delano Roosevelt's presidential election on a platform called the New Deal.

In 1933, the constitutional amendment to end Prohibition was passed, and Gimbels was ready with a full stock of spirits to meet the demand. On the day after repeal, one Gimbels employee tallied $200,000 worth of liquor sales.

Schuster's

Schuster's survived the challenges of the Depression by promoting heavily, using flexible staffing to keep its sales force and offering its employees incentives. In 1933, Albert T. Friedman died, and his son Max Friedman took over the management of the store. Max Friedman used part-time workers for staffing flexibility and to minimize layoff of regular staff. In 1930, Schuster's had 3,700 employees working in its three stores and warehouse. Of these, 1,269 were full-time "insured" employees. In 1934, *Schuster's Weekly* advertised its 50th Anniversary Sale on Monday, April 16 (touting Hershey's Kisses for twenty-one cents per pound and free parking), claiming it had more than 5,000 employees and they were there to serve the customers. It is unclear how many of the 5,000 represented full time, but Schuster's did hire part-time help to cover its busiest times.

Schuster's reduced store hours in 1931 by closing on Saturday afternoons in July and August, touting this as giving its employees an extra half day off during the nice summer months. Furlough days and reduced hours for the employees gave them a steady income in these difficult times.

New employees were first trained on store systems and salesmanship and then matched with a sponsor who provided additional training. Articles in the monthly employee magazine *Keeping in Touch* gave tips on approaching customers, dealing with different kinds of customers and suggestion selling. "Want slips" were used to keep track of out-of-stock items that customers requested. Employees were urged to write down their suggestions for improvements to the store and turn them in. The store superintendent would meet with employees to discuss their suggestions, and the top two or three suggestions would be printed in *K.I.T.*

In the 1930s, Schuster's sales promotions included the Annual Sale, the Semi-Annual Sale, the End-of-the-Month Sale, the Anniversary Sale, Rummage Sales and Economy Day Sales. *Schuster's Weekly* was expanded to ten to twenty pages, depending on the promotion, and a page of general interest was added. One interesting ad promoting three bath towels for eighty-five cents used the headline "Let's give all Milwaukee a chance to take a bath with a real towel value." Word-of-mouth advertising was also used. Employees were asked to talk to their friends and relatives and invite them to the store to take advantage of the big sales. Prizes were given to those employees who brought in the most customers.

Schuster's introduced its own credit cards, called Charga-Plates, in 1938. These were metal cards that were inserted into an imprinter at each register and recorded the customer's name, address and account information on the sales checks. In the 1930s, Schuster's also expanded its savings stamp program to grocery stores and meat markets.

The electrical appliance department was an eclectic mix of large and small appliances, with refrigerators, washing machines, dishwashers, machines that did the ironing, irons, percolators, toasters and popcorn poppers. A model kitchen was installed in the basement of the Third Street store, and customers were promised help in finding in the store any utensil that was used in the cooking demonstrations. The delicatessen featured 108 varieties of cheese, Scandinavian treats, S&W Fine Food canned vegetables and Viking Herring snacks. Schuster's was tremendously proud of its stores and offered guided tours to its customers that included a tour of the boiler room.

Schuster's continued to offer a wide range of benefits to its employees, including paying employees a 1 percent commission weekly of net sales if the sales quota was met. The dress code for saleswomen called for a long-sleeved dress with an even hemline, cape collar and either a white or eggshell blouse. The Twelfth Street store had a silence room that had plenty of comfortable cots and was a great place for employees to take a noontime nap. The store provided umbrellas to its employees if the weather turned rainy when they walked home for lunch. Women were at the bottom of the hierarchy. A note in the Gimbel Collection for a Mitchell Street store open house said that the presenters talked too long, the PA system was too loud and male executives with good voices should be used instead of female employees.

Social activities promoted a strong sense of loyalty. By 1939, the Schuster's Activities Association Board structure consisted of more than 50 members, with an executive council, a general chairman and 4 council chairmen representing the three stores and the warehouse, with subcommittees of basketball, baseball, golf, tennis, bowling, ping-pong, acting and self-education. The *Schafkopf* (sheep head, a German card game) Poultry Tournament gave winners prizes of turkeys, geese and ducks. Employees could choose to participate in a ping-pong team tournament, take an evening cruise on the lake, join a tennis or bowling tournament or sign up for an educational tour of the city. Band music was losing its popularity, and Schuster's no longer allowed the band to practice on store time. In 1958, 225 of those hired during the Depression celebrated their membership in the twenty-five-year club.

BILLIE THE BROWNIE UPDATE

Probably the most memorable of Schuster's promotions was its Billie the Brownie character. Radio was a popular form of entertainment during the Depression, and in 1930 Larry Teich started *Our Club* and became Captain Larry. Children sang, recited poetry and performed on the air. On November 8, 1931, Teich broadcast his first *Billie the Brownie* program on WTMJ radio, featuring Captain Larry, Billie and Santa Claus. The *Billie the Brownie* radio program was the first sponsored radio program on a Milwaukee radio station. Schuster's sponsored *Billie the Brownie* for twenty-four more years, ending the program in 1955. Schuster's was also the first advertiser to sign up when Channel 4 television started broadcasting in 1947. Teich used the same format he had developed for *Our Club* for *Billie the Brownie*, telling stories, reading children's letters to Santa and keeping everyone informed about Santa's progress.

The first two weeks of the show featured the trip from the North Pole to Milwaukee. Teich made his own sound effects, creating a lot of static in the background while Santa was on the road. Another sound effect was Billie's dog, Willie Wagtail, barking to tell the children's dogs that they were not to interrupt Santa when he visited the children's homes on Christmas Eve. Frenetic activity in Santa's Toy Shop would raise the listening children's

Billie the Brownie. *Photo courtesy of Paul Geenen, original statue provided by Jack Koplin.*

hopes that they would soon be seeing their Christmas wishes. The Christmas Eve show was the season's finale, and Santa would load his sleigh with a lot of grunting, pounding and background conversation. The show was interactive, as children were asked to shout that they were good before Billie opened the storybook and read.

The show was broadcast daily for seven weeks, and as many as ninety-four thousand children sent their letters to Santa at a rate of ten thousand or more a week. These would be put in a large drum, and a dozen letters would be pulled from the drum and read over the air each day. A postcard with the following message was sent in response to every letter received: "Dear David [name written by hand], Santa, Me-Tik, Reindeer and Schuster's wish you a Merry Christmas. We all enjoyed reading your letter and hope to see you [at Schuster's] before Christmas. Love, Billie the Brownie." Sometimes, children would write asking for food, clothing and toys. According to Gurda, bulk quantities of food were supplied at outdoor relief stations; people carrying their food home in their child's coaster wagon referred to this as "pulling the wagon." Schuster's sent a letter in return suggesting that the families contact the Family Welfare Department, although there were many more families in need than the safety net could take care of.

On Christmas Eve, children left a bone for Willie Wagtail, milk and cookies for Santa and Billie and sugar for the reindeer. This created such a demand for bones that butchers saved the tastier bones for Christmas Eve use. The Christmas parade itself continued to be a big success, and Billie the Brownie continued to be the star of the parade. The handmade wooden figures of Billie and other characters in the story were stored in sturdy, hand-crafted wooden crates during the off-season.

The last *Billie the Brownie* show was on December 24, 1955. Television was becoming popular, and radio was losing its hold. Schuster's tried to adapt the concept to television but found that it was difficult and expensive and, after a few tries, retired Billie.

TIMELINE

1930	Schuster's builds its service building on Commerce Street
November 8, 1931	The first *Billie the Brownie* program airs
1933	Albert Friedman dies, and his son Max takes over Schuster's
1936	Charlie Zadok takes over as vice-president and general manager of Gimbels
1936	Gimbels remodels its first floor, builds Tasty Town and installs escalators

CHAPTER 5

War and Peace

1940–1950

"DOWN BY SCHUSTER'S BUT TWO BLOCKS"

Even during World War II, Schuster's continued to provide creative benefits to attract and keep its customers. Free and convenient parking was a feature of all Schuster's stores, and every parking lot featured a tower staffed with an attendant who would indicate to customers where the empty parking spots were. The Mitchell Street store was expanded in 1941 with a delicatessen and a new lunch counter that seated over seventy-five people, and in the basement, two new "spacious stairways" led to the newly redone "air cooled" housewares department. The air conditioning was a series of pumps, pipes and vents that drew air over a water system to cool the store. In 1941, the Third Street store was expanded, and a new rotary phone system went live in all the stores.

The shortages caused by the war meant that Schuster's was not able to use the words "Sale" or "Special Value" in any of its promotions, as these words were seen as encouraging panic buying. A detailed *Air Raid Protection* manual calling for wardens at every floor was drawn up because of the fear of the country's enemies mounting a successful air attack. A meal-planning guide titled *The Health for Victory Club* encouraged homemakers to make nutritious meals from locally grown foods. Service members were sent food boxes every other month containing "fudge, stationary [*sic*], chewy cookies, flashlights and nuts," according to *Keeping in Touch*. On Mother's Day, Schuster's sent plants to employee mothers with sons in the service.

The success of Schuster's most popular promotion continued. In fact, Schuster's and WTMJ had an agreement that war news would not preempt any children's radio shows, so *Billie the Brownie* continued without any interruption during the holiday seasons of the war years. The Christmas parade was held every year, and in 1947, the *Milwaukee Journal* reported that 300,000 people lined the nine-mile route that snaked past all three Schuster's stores.

Schuster's worked hard to keep its employees happy. Dancing and card playing followed the Schuster's Activities Association annual awards banquet. The store monitored employee participation in sports and was careful to make sure that their efforts were improving employee loyalty. Many sports were showing a decline, although tennis was increasing by 15 percent. Management did worry about the fact that more men than women participated in the sporting activities, although women made up 75 to 80 percent of the workforce. Employees looked forward to the 20 percent discount offered for three days during November and were encouraged to do their Christmas shopping early. These employee retention efforts paid off. Photos of 84 people who were in the twenty-five-year club, including 21 new inductees, were featured in the May 1945 issue of *Keeping in Touch*. Schuster's had 1,699 full-time employees and 3,447 total employees in 1943. In 1946, Schuster's followed the national trend of a forty-hour workweek by reducing its workweek from forty-five hours.

Schuster's had been buying up land in the area bound by Fond du Lac Avenue, Sixtieth Street and Capital Drive since the early 1940s, and by the early '50s, Schuster's owned all of it except a small parcel in the southeastern corner. The sixty-five-acre site was the "golden triangle" that offered all the parking a new Schuster's store would need. This was to be the site of Schuster's next store; in March 1952, Schuster's announced its plans to build a new shopping center named Capital Court.

GIMBELS DURING THE WAR

The war also changed the way Gimbels approached its business. Gimbels' customers could buy hard-to-find items when other stores were sold out because Bernard Gimbel negotiated a $21 million credit line before the war and used it to buy merchandise that was thought to be in short supply, including $3.5 million worth of women's nylon stockings. Textiles were rationed, and Gimbels' salespeople made sure that customers only purchased what was absolutely needed. Helene Furst, who worked in Tasty Town in 1943, remembers not being allowed to drink Coke because it was reserved "for the boys."

Gimbels supported the war in many ways. Monthly articles in the employee newsletters honored its numerous men and women who were serving in the armed services, calling them our stalwart heroes "who have left us to take a crack at the Axis."

The Broadcaster published letters, mailing addresses and photos from the men and women in the service. The names of all the Gimbels employees engaged in military service were posted on a sign in the store titled "In Honor of Gimbel Men and Women in Service." In January 1944, Gimbels had its Fourth War Loan Drive, and each employee was asked to sell $200 worth of war bonds by February 15. The "Blood Donors Honor Roll" listed those who gave blood, and employees were reminded that their blood donation might mean that there was "one less name on the Casualty list." Huge stacks of jars of homemade fruit and vegetables were collected to feed the ten thousand service members who frequented the USO located on North Water Street in Milwaukee. The store collected empty boxes and bundled them into bales for recycling. One employee wrote in *The Broadcaster* that she thought about "my own overseas soldier" every time she broke down a carton for recycling. Gimbels collected contributions for the Red Cross efforts in Russia and France and was host to the official war exhibit of the Polish government in exile in London. According to *The Broadcaster*, an exhibit about the Dutch underground that contained "official war paintings and photographs…captured war material…and the bloodstained flying suit of a Nazis aviator" was a "thrilling war exhibit, showing the way the dauntless Dutch fight back!"

Recruiting staff during the war was a constant challenge. A 1943 issue of *The Broadcaster* suggested that one was helping the war effort by working for Gimbels because "the distribution of goods to busy war-time workers is considered vital and necessary service." This was a nice way to perform a "patriotic service," as well as earn some Christmas money. Experienced workers were asked to mentor new employees, and in 1943, a suggestion system was implemented with representatives from the store management, publicity, control and personnel reviewing entries. The best suggestions were given a two-dollar award.

The Broadcaster employee newsletters of the 1940s described the store's employees and their duties. The "elevator girls" had the skills

Tuesday, September 10, 1940, Gimbels' Founders Day advertisement. *Photo courtesy of Paul Geenen, newspaper advertisement supplied by Bud Schneider.*

for the "smooth manipulation of cars, [making] accurate landings," while watching "for hands and feet, and scurrying customers." The print shop employees were experienced in running the Addressograph and the Graphotype. The twelve "hello girls" juggled incoming calls from 69 trunk lines and connected them to 250 telephone extensions. Employees were asked to use the "little red store book" to save time for the operators. The order board wrote up customers' phone orders and sent them to the selling floor to be filled. The "Parkettes" offered valet parking to Gimbels customers.

The advertising department had eleven artists who drew the illustrations and two layout "girls" who put the ads together. The Eighth Floor Restaurant staff of fifty could really "dish it out." The eight "day maids" kept the store looking good. The sign shop's four card machine operators and a skilled artist who hand brushed the large signs produced the signage for the store. Six stenographers in the mail-order and order board department wrote customers letters requesting clarification on orders. The employees of the candy kitchen were part of an experienced crew of thirty-two people who made three thousand pounds of candy daily for sale in the first-floor candy department.

Workers were in short supply, and Gimbels recognized those who stayed. In 1945 and 1946, members of the Gimbels' twenty-five-year club enjoyed a sit-down dinner served on white tablecloths for 1,800 people at the Milwaukee Auditorium. Chicken was served, local beers were featured at the open bar and two bands played music for people to dance to after dinner. Miss Elizabeth Koepcke, from fourth-floor woolens, celebrated her fiftieth anniversary at one of these events.

Members of the twenty-five-year club touted the benefits of working at Gimbels: sick pay, vacations, employee discounts, employee lounge and a cafeteria that served modestly priced meals. Again, following the trend in the country after the war, employees' workweeks were shortened from forty-five hours to forty hours. Bowling and basketball teams were organized, and forty men and forty women competed in mixed bowling matches at the Antlers Alleys. The store's first men's basketball team practiced at Lapham Park Social Center and the Juneau High School gym. They played the company teams of Golden Guernsey, the Veterans' Administration, Falk Corporation and Crucible Steel. The team's award dinner was held at the Tic-Toc-Club.

Gimbels leadership received national attention in 1945 when *Fortune* magazine ran a feature article about Bernard F. Gimbel, highlighting the four Gimbels stores in New York, Philadelphia, Pittsburgh and Milwaukee and the five Saks stores in New York, Chicago, Palm Beach, Miami Beach and Beverly Hills.

Gimbels Milwaukee executives garnered attention from their employees as well. In 1944, Charles Zadok, the Milwaukee store's vice-president and general manager, spoke at the 102nd anniversary kick-off meeting and "gave an address which was interrupted time after time by ovations from his co-workers."

The Broadcaster was equally impressed in describing a Gimbels Milwaukee executive, merchandise manager Howard E. Kaufman. He was described as "a popular man…But don't let the mild exterior lead you too far astray, for if you do, you might stub your toe hard on the solid rock-bed underneath. His job is often a tough one, and he is fully equal to it when it gets that way." A merchandise manager was glorified as having a higher calling, as "it was always the merchant who served mankind as the carrier of civilization, the distributor of new inventions and discoveries." Publicity director Raymond F. Keift said, "Advertising…must reflect…a store's real ability to serve the many wants of the community."

AFTER THE WAR

After the war came to an end, Gimbels connected with a local event that became a national story and a symbol of postwar hope. In April 1945, a mallard duck made her nest on the top of a hollowed-out wood piling in the Milwaukee River near the Wisconsin Avenue bridge. *Milwaukee Journal's* outdoor writer, Gordon MacQuardrie, wrote a story with the headline "Mallard Sets an Eggs-Ample in a 'Penthouse' 10 Feet Up" and named the duck Gertie. The world press picked up the story of Gertie's tenacity in hatching her eggs on this shaky pedestal as a sign of hope during the challenging times that followed World War II.

The City of Milwaukee postponed replacing the deteriorating piling, and the Humane Society placed a worker nearby to guard the nest from being disturbed. Pedestrians gathered at the bridge railing, and motorists blocked traffic to get a peek. *Life* magazine ran a photo spread about Gertie, and Eddie Cantor included the duck in his act. Gertie got a mail sack full of Mother's Day cards, and the clerk of Milwaukee County issued birth certificates for her brood. The bridge tender, Paul Benn, and his companion rowed their

Gertie the duck statue on the Wisconsin Avenue bridge. *Courtesy of Paul Geenen.*

small boat onto the rushing river and rescued one of the ducklings that had fallen in after a spring storm.

Gimbels capitalized on Gertie's popularity, putting Gertie and her ducklings for two days in a display window on Wisconsin Avenue before releasing them. Milwaukeeans trooped downtown to see the ducks in Gimbels' window before the entire family was relocated to the lagoon on the lakefront; Gimbels and Gertie have been connected ever since. In 1946, *The Broadcaster* wrote that the "Gertie" float in Milwaukee's Centurama Parade stole the show.

Another memorable Gimbels promotion during the 1940s was *The Adventures of Gimbie and Ellie*, which was broadcast over WISN daily from November to Christmas. The adventures of two elephants traveling from the North Pole to Milwaukee were Gimbels' answer to Schuster's Billie the Brownie. A promoter by the name of Will Hill brought his dancing elephants, Gimbie and Ellie, along with ponies and performing dogs, to Gimbels to thrill Milwaukee's children. There is not a lot of information available on where this show was held, although there is anecdotal evidence that the show was held on the eighth floor near the restaurant. Leon Boniface, Gimbels' longtime display director from the early 1960s on, thought that the waste produced by the elephants and ponies made it more probable that the show was held on the fourth floor in the toy department.

Gimbels started numerous construction projects after the war. In 1947, Bernard Gimbel, president of Gimbel Brothers, toured the Milwaukee Gimbels store and commented favorably on the new seven-hundred-car parking garage built at the corner of Michigan and Plankington. The flagship store had a new bright look, sales floors were air conditioned, escalators were installed on the south end of the building and the fifth-floor furniture and the sixth-floor china, glassware and lamp departments were remodeled. Model rooms in the new furniture departments featured the California look, with upholstering in "an exciting panorama of lime, shrimp, steel grey, chartreuse and beige" colors. After the war, affordable housing was in short supply, and low-cost experimental housing was promoted as a way of meeting the needs of returning GIs who were forming families and settling down. Gimbels' interior designers decorated a steel, factory-made house named the Harmon House.

Gimbels took advantage of new technology, including "The Legometer," which measured women's legs to ensure a correct fit in hosiery. Promotions were added to take advantage of all the families that were being formed, with the 1949 Bridal Show breaking all records. Gimbels' fashion leadership was promoted by teens from the local high schools who met twice a month as the high school fashion board and modeled in the ready-to-wear departments, the Eighth Floor Restaurant and fashion shows.

Art was popular again after the war, and in 1948 and 1949, Gimbels sponsored a juried show of over thirty Wisconsin artists. New homes needed flowers, and the Gimbels flower shop was rated of the top ten flower departments in the country's department stores. In November 1945, the National Rose Show was held on Gimbels' fourth floor, with florists from both Gimbels and the community at large organizing the show.

Tasty Town was generating a lot of traffic. Banana splits and strawberry shortcakes were bestsellers, part of the 1,600 orders the employees filled every day for sundaes, sodas and malts. In 1948, Ruth Scherer, the Tasty Town manager, reported that the restaurant consumed over one hundred gallons of ice cream on an average day.

Gimbels increased its training efforts. In 1946, Gimbels' new training department showed a movie on customer service titled *By Jupiter!* to nine hundred Gimbels employees. A job simplification course was offered to "assistant buyers, non-selling department heads, buyers and floor supervisors," according to *The Broadcaster*. "Have You Eye Appeal?" was the theme of a good grooming campaign. Salespeople were asked to wear tailored and conservative clothes and leave their sequins and hair ornaments at home.

In 1949, Joseph A. Rapkin and Robert A. "Bob" Polacheck went to Buffalo, Cleveland, St. Louis and New York to visit newly built regional shopping centers. Rapkin asked Kurtis R. Froedtert, owner of Froedtert Malt Company and one of Rapkin's law firm clients, to purchase thirty acres for the new Southgate Shopping Center on the south side of Milwaukee. By 1951, Southgate had twenty-two stores.

Gimbels broke ground for its new store at Southgate on July 27, 1953. The baby boomer generation was coming on the scene, and the bridal shows, marriage and then the baby boom were creating demand for new suburbs and freeways, causing both Gimbels and Schuster's to offer new shopping venues in the form of branch stores to attract their customers.

TIMELINE

1941	Oscar Greenwald dies
1941	Schuster's expands its Third Street store to its present size
1941	Schuster's expands its Mitchell Street store to its present size
Spring 1945	Gertie the duck nests on a piling in the river near Gimbels
1945	*Fortune* magazine runs a feature article on Bernard Gimbel

1947   Gimbels opens its parking pavilion at Plankington and
                Michigan

1948   Gimbels remodels its fifth-floor furniture departments

1949   Gimbels remodels its sixth-floor lamp and china
                departments

CHAPTER 6

Branch Stores

1950–1960

I CAME TO WORK CHRISTMAS AND STAYED TWENTY-FIVE YEARS

Gimbels was a good place to work. It was good because of the people, who worked together and often became lifelong friends. The camaraderie among the employees was amazing. The culture of people's associations with each other was something that human resource managers dream about. It was built over a long period of time, and it is unclear how it could be re-created. This was a dream job to many associates. The associates had a good understanding of what their responsibilities were and were very good at what they did. People stayed, and employee turnover among the full-time workers was very low.

Part-time regulars who worked a minimum of twenty hours a week received regular benefits, including health insurance, discounts on merchandise and vacations. Employees received good healthcare from three visiting nurses, and a physician kept regular office hours at the store. Regular employees received two weeks of vacation after working a full year, three weeks after working seven years and four weeks after working twenty years.

The employee magazine, the *Gimbelite*, published ten months out of the year, ran articles about the men and women serving in the Korean War, the bowling team scores of the men's and women's teams and news about the thirty-eight-member Gimbel chorus. Prize-winning apple pies baked by

Downtown Milwaukee sometime in the 1950s. *Courtesy of Jack Koplin.*

Caroline Siegel and oil paintings by Hazel Gehrke were topics of interest in the employee magazine.

Working at Gimbels could be a family tradition. Three generations of Hattie Herz's family were Gimbels employees, with Hattie starting in 1887, her daughter Selda working in accounting, and her grandson Harold Loebel completing eighteen years in 1950. In 1952, the *Gimbelite* featured four Gimbels employee couples, and in 1958, it profiled five employee couples and four pairs of employee siblings.

Membership in the twenty-five-year club was a goal sought by many, with one to two dozen employees joining every year during this decade. In 1956, Hanah Winter, accommodations desk supervisor, and Alice Sullivan, timekeeper, retired after more than fifty years at Gimbels. In 1900, Winter had started as a transfer girl, and in 1901, at the age of twelve, Sullivan had started as a cash girl. Frances Mareth, marking supervisor, worked for the store over sixty years. In 1956, almost one-third of all Gimbels' full-time employees, a total of 558, were members of either the ten- or twenty-five-year club. Gimbels' employees had a strong loyalty toward each other from working together for so long.

People raised families on their Gimbels salaries. Employees stayed, although they were paid minimum wage, were given average benefits and stood on their feet all day. They did like the 10 to 20 percent merchandise discount. Hannah Isaacs, a coats and suits salesperson, started at Gimbels in 1942. A single parent with seven children, she put her five boys and two girls through college with the help of her Gimbels salary and the GI Bill of Rights.

Gimbels continued to work hard to solidify employee loyalty. It held an annual store party at the Eagles Club on Wisconsin Avenue, where many of the four thousand Gimbelites who attended danced past midnight to two bands in George Devine's Million Dollar Ballroom. Card games were played in the Aerie Room. Holiday parties with games of chance, popcorn balls, taffy and noisemakers were held other years on the eighth floor of the store. Themes varied from Western to Hawaiian.

Departments enjoyed socializing. Individual selling and service departments held their own Christmas breakfasts. Christmas parties were held for the children of employees and customers, with acts such as the "International Whirling Aces" by Jerry Wagner, a member of the stock department, and his daughter. Rocking horses, wagons and cars from the toy department were available for children to try out.

Opposite top: Mary Off's retirement party in 1951. *Left to right*: Charlie Andrews, chief electrician; Al De Both, maintenance mechanic; Mary Off, housekeeping; Joe Ver Luga (standing), carpenter; Laurence Dickelman, maintenance supervisor; Joe ?, carpenter; ? Lenatz, porter; Christ Schoberth, carpenter foreman; Charlie Lang, carpenter; Mary ?, housekeeping forelady; Frank Manthe, housekeeping and maintenance manager. *Courtesy of Harold Badzinski.*

Opposite bottom: John Fitzgerald's retirement party in the Terrace Room of the Eighth Floor Restaurant in the early 1950s. *From left, front*: unknown; unknown; Henry Wurm, cabinetmaker foreman; unknown; Frank Kroll, cabinetmaker; unknown; unknown; Al De Both, maintenance mechanic; John Fitzgerald, cabinetmaker, and his wife. *Rear*: Ed Heider, electrician; Charlie Andrews, chief electrician; John Gerova, electrician; Dick Cerny, electrician; Al Blanchard, chief draftsman. *From front right*: Frank Manthe, housekeeping and maintenance manager; Christ Schoberth, carpenter foreman; Harry Powers, electrician; Harry Badzinski, draftsman; Harold Wanserski, cabinetmaker; Laurence Dickelman, maintenance supervisor. *Courtesy of Harold Badzinski.*

Employees took care of each other. In 1956, Gimbels employees carpooled or walked in during the seven-day transit strike to staff the store. And they were loyal. It took Ann Jaeckels three hours to walk from Eighty-fifth and North Avenue to come to work during the strike.

The store provided smartly tailored uniforms to its elevator operators and waitresses. In 1950, the winter uniforms of the elevator operators were dark green wool gabardine suits, and in summer, their uniforms were made of aqua-colored Sacony cloth, both made in women's alterations. Tasty Town apprentice waitresses wore gray uniforms until they had a month's experience, when they were given the blue nylon uniforms of the regular wait staff.

Sales were tallied to determine trends. Ed Danaher, the manager of the main aisle, compiled the daily sales report at 5:45 p.m. using each department's sales reports. The next day, Margaret Weier completed a report showing each department's sales and the weather, comparing that year to the previous year. Each Friday, the statistics department generated a report that told the merchants the number of dollars they had to spend. Operating statements that detailed net sales and profit for each department were published monthly.

Gimbels saw the importance of a highly trained staff. The Flying Squad was a group of salespeople able to work in any department that needed help, from corsets to shoes. Seventeen men and women worked in men's alterations. They started as tailors' apprentices in Europe, where they worked for room and board for three years before becoming journeymen and immigrating to the United States.

Gimbels was known for its delicatessen. Meats and sausages from Weisels, Usingers and Thieles filled a good part of its ninety feet of refrigerated cases. Fresh ham salad made daily from the baked ham ends was only one of the many salads offered. Swiss cheese made to Gimbels' specifications was a bestseller. The delicatessen would sell at least four eight-hundred-pound tubs of Swiss cheese daily during storewide sales. Popular cheese gift boxes were assembled in a staging area during the Christmas season. John Uschan, the delicatessen manager, took inventory every evening before he went home and placed orders with the kitchen and the local vendors so that the deli cases would be full the next morning when the store opened.

The men of housekeeping worked with the store electricians, painters and carpenters to set up special events. They set up the runways, stages, chairs and PA system for the fashion shows and other gatherings. The female housekeeping staff took a break from cleaning the store every evening and had a 9:00 p.m. meal together in Tasty Town.

GIMBELS PROMOTIONS

Seasonal displays put Gimbels customers in the mood to buy. The display department drew up the designs for Toyland, the Trim-a-Tree shop and Santa's throne in July. Displays for the main aisles and the ledges behind the sales islands were also decided upon. Shop crews and electricians assembled the Christmas windows at tremendous cost. The Saturday night and all day Sunday before Thanksgiving, the entire display department worked to get the selling floors and the windows trimmed and ready. A Christmas display featuring animated George Silvestri figures for the bank of downtown windows opened on Thanksgiving Eve.

Gimbels supported local artists; for example, in 1951, Charles Zadok, vice-president and general manager, conceived the idea for "Wisconsin Airscapes and Landscapes" while on a flight over Holland. The winners of this annual art collection were provided a box of crayons and a sketch pad to draw with on an airplane ride over the countryside. Later, in 1959, Gimbels donated sixty-eight paintings by Wisconsin artists accumulated over the years to the Milwaukee Art Center.

The postwar families were moving to the new houses going up in the suburbs. In 1951, the $10 million regional Southgate Shopping Center opened. Kurtis R. Froedtert, owner of the Froedtert Malt Company, had supplied the funds for this new shopping center. It was the first of its kind in Milwaukee, opening with an assortment of small stores clustered around an open-air mall. The largest tenant at the time, Krambo Supermarket, had success with night openings, and by 1952, all the stores in the Southgate mall were open for six evenings. By 1953, Southgate was enjoying a 30 percent increase in sales, and the center employed over five hundred people. It was showing impressive growth and looked like a good location for a Gimbels store.

Gimbels opened its first branch store at Southgate in 1954, and 4,000 Gimbels employees and their families toured the store at the employee open house in late September. Charles Zadok said that many customers would take public transit to this new store because the day was distant when every family would have a second car for "the wife to use for shopping." On October 1, 1954, Mayor Frank P. Zeidler cut the ribbon for Gimbels' $5 million Southgate store while 1,500 people watched, huddling under the cantilevered outside canopy to escape the rain. The transit system ran a full-page advertisement detailing the new bus routes that served the mall.

A Gimbels ad quoted John Keats in describing its store at the Southgate mall as "a thing of beauty and joy forever." The comfortable rubber tile floor and the modern murals, such as the fish design in the sporting goods department, were aesthetics that would be sure to please the customers. The "fresh-as-a-Lake-breeze" air conditioning would make customers comfortable, and the "silken smooth" escalators would effortlessly carry everyone to every department in the store. The shoe department was decorated with a mural of old shoes and had fashionable but uncomfortable-looking wrought-iron and leather chairs for its customers. Zadok, with his European background, was the inspiration for the tan and cream Italian marble that lined the escalator tunnels.

The new store offered the same merchandise and service offerings as Gimbels' downtown store. The store was staffed with people from the neighborhood, and the employees stayed. Gimbels' Southgate store had a large number of people in the ten- and twenty-five-year clubs of later years. Southgate had its own Christmas party, with bingo, card playing and dancing, just like the downtown store. It was held at the nearby Our Lady Queen of Peace Church.

In 1956, Charles Zadok was named Gimbel Brothers' new vice-president in charge of expansion. His new office would handle all the new stores being built by Gimbel Brothers at its four locations. Zadok contracted much of the design work to outside firms due to the number of stores that were being built at the four Gimbel Brothers divisions. In that same year, Maurice Berger became head of Gimbels Milwaukee.

Gimbels in Milwaukee had skilled in-store cabinetmakers, electricians, carpenters and painters. In 1956, these craftsmen installed new fixtures, lighting and a tiled floor in the Economy Basement Store, now called simply the Basement Store. In 1959, new food preparation and holding fixtures were installed in Tasty Town to speed the service of the restaurant's popular sandwiches and fountain items. Walls in the restaurant were removed, drop ceilings were installed and the counter area was opened up.

In September 1958, Mayfair Mall, then called Westgate, opened as a central open-air mall similar in design to Capital Court and Southgate. Three thousand people attended the opening ceremonies of Gimbels'

Tasty Town in 1959. *Courtesy of Milwaukee County Historical Society.*

Mayfair store. The photos of the Gimbels Mayfair store interiors show that it was lightly stocked and had large, open areas with either carpeting or striped dark and light tile floors. The store entrances were at two levels because of the rolling terrain of the site. Pneumatic tubes were used to make change for the cash registers. Only twenty-two stores were leased out of the seventy stores planned, and the other anchor department store, Marshall Field's, was scheduled for completion after the upcoming Christmas season.

SCHUSTER'S EMPLOYEES

Longtime employees recruited new talent for Schuster's. In 1952, Jack Koplin responded to a Schuster's advertisement for an accounts receivable clerk, even though his father-in-law, a forty-six-year employee and a buyer for Schuster's, warned him that retail was stressful. On March 17, 1952,

Koplin was hired as an accounts receivable assistant. In 1956, Koplin was in charge of accounts payable and was responsible for managing a small staff. The new Capital Court store was opening, and Koplin's department was responsible for matching receiving records with invoices and issuing checks to Schuster's vendors. Koplin worked twelve-hour days, six days a week for six months, wrestling with the flood of paperwork caused by the successful new store.

Marie L. Olivier started at the Twelfth and Vliet store as a cook in the deli kitchen in 1948 and moved to the Third Street store a few years later. An African American who passed as white, her ethnicity was not questioned until her brown-skinned daughter, Frances Bryant, visited her mom at the Third Street store. Marie was a single mom with thirteen children and worked at Schuster's until she retired in 1974. She was very proud of being "the first person of black blood to retire from Schuster's." Her daughter remembers with fondness the good meals they enjoyed using the leftovers her mom brought home from the deli kitchen.

Schuster's continued to build a loyal, highly trained workforce. About forty people graduated from Schuster's Junior Executive training program annually. Supervisors would recommend candidates for the training program, which was for those on a buyer, assistant buyer or floor manager track. Most of the trainees who participated in this program were from the stores, with only a few being new hires. The training consisted of classroom training as well as rotating assignments in a variety of departments.

Schuster's also held fashion clinics for its own salespeople. After a general presentation on fashion trends, the buyers would lead break-out sessions for the salespeople.

The SAA (Schuster's Athletic Association) continued to offer a wide variety of activities to its employees. Koplin remembers with fondness playing on baseball, bowling and basketball teams. He also played ping-pong and enjoyed a round or two of golf with his fellow workers.

SCHUSTER'S PROMOTIONS

In the early 1950s, Schuster's promotional approach closely reflected the European heritage of its customers. The wine and liquor shop at the Third Street store carried forty different kinds of scotch and a wide assortment of local and imported beers. People flocked to get German specialty dishes such as the herring in wine sauce in the delicatessen and stollen and fruitcakes made with sherry and brandy in the bakery.

Schuster's experimented with new selling techniques such as Quick Service Desks in 1952. This new concept had been first tried in some stores on the East Coast, where it was used to save time for the salespeople and make shopping easier for the customer. Cash registers were placed in the center of the selling areas, replacing individual department sales desks. Signs were placed near displays encouraging customers to take their purchases to the Quick Service Desks.

In the early 1950s, the Amana Family Food Plan invited families to buy choice meats, Birds Eye and Snow Crop fruits and vegetables with an Amana freezer. Meals would be made ahead by the customer and then frozen for later.

On September 9, 1953, Schuster's invited over two hundred business leaders and officials to be part of the groundbreaking ceremony for Capital Court. Schuster's catering department prepared a smorgasbord of platters of salad, raw beef, strip sirloin, *spanferkels*, turkey, ham, vegetables, potatoes au gratin, French pastries and coffee for the guests.

Capital Court opened on August 28, 1956, on a hot day that tested its new air conditioning, according to the *Milwaukee Sentinel*. Schuster's, JCPenney and Chapman's were the anchor department stores, and more than fifty small stores were completed on both sides of the open mall. Only twenty leased stores opened on the first day, but the thought was that the center would eventually employ three thousand people.

Capital Court was the "dream" shopping center, according to a large ad that ran in the *Milwaukee Journal*. The center was easy to reach by bus or car, and customers could window-shop in comfort in the shade of a canopy. Displays would draw customers in to a wide selection of merchandise. Despite the rain, an outdoor fashion show went on during the entire opening day.

Walter Kroening, assistant general director of Capital Court Shopping Center, saw the new shopping center as being a large department store. He assembled retail stores that offered a wide and varied selection of merchandise. Kroening chose tenants that would give the center a good mix of merchandise, selecting tenants based on their merchandise offerings. Many stores approached him asking to lease space next to Schuster's. He controlled selling conditions in the mall—for example, requiring the popcorn wagon to sell unbuttered popcorn so customers' buttery hands would not soil the merchandise in the stores.

In a 1953 speech, Kroening said that the traffic planning done for the center embraced "all of its forms, pedestrian, private car, truck and public carrier." It is unclear whether the planners of Capital Court were aware of community resistance to completing the plans for freeways in Milwaukee, which resulted in Capital Court having poor freeway access.

The retail picture was changing with the new expressways. In 1958, Southgate's trading area had shown a 34 percent increase in population, surpassing the general growth in Milwaukee by 13 percent, according to the *Milwaukee Journal Study of Shopping Habits*. Southgate and Capital Court were attracting big numbers of new shoppers. Capital Court was one of the most successful shopping centers in the entire country during this time. The sales increases from Capital Court came at the expense of Schuster's Mitchell Street, Third Street and Twelfth Street stores.

In 1958, with the new Capital Court store, Schuster's reached a sales volume of $50 million, a high-water mark for the company. It consistently was generating more than a 2 percent after-tax profit that was divided between the stockholders, and the balance was used to fund its expansion plans. Schuster's stock was held by a small group of people, including members of the Friedman family, employees and local residents. None had deep pockets, and the company depended on sales growth to finance expansion.

Max Friedman, the CEO of Schuster's, died unexpectedly in 1954, and his brother, Ralph Friedman, replaced Max as CEO. The Milwaukee retail market was getting more competitive, Ralph Friedman was getting older and both of his sons were not involved in the business. One son raced sports cars, and the other enjoyed a musical career. Unfortunately, there was no successor for Ralph Friedman in sight.

TIMELINE

March 31, 1954	Max Friedman dies and his brother Ralph takes over Schuster's
September 28, 1954	Gimbels opens Southgate
December 24, 1955	The last *Billie the Brownie* radio show airs

Milwaukee's Beloved Department Stores

1956	Charles Zadok moves to New York to manage the expansion of stores in all Gimbels divisions
1956	Maurice Berger becomes the new executive head of Gimbels
August 28, 1956	Schuster's opens Capital Court Shopping Center
1958	Gimbels opens its store in Mayfair shopping center
1959	Gimbels remodels Tasty Town
1959	Schuster's discontinues Schuster's Stamps
1960	Gimbels remodels Tasty Town
1960	Gimbels starts its Fashion Forum
November 1960	Schuster's Christmas parade ends

CHAPTER 7

The Growth of Suburbs

1960–1970

GIMBELS BUYS SCHUSTER'S

The urban landscape was changing. Freeways were making it easy for people to move to the suburbs. Manufacturing companies were moving beyond Milwaukee, taking central city jobs with them. Inner-city neighborhoods were declining. As cities grew outward in 1960, Schuster's planned three new stores: Packard Plaza on the south side of Milwaukee, Hilldale in the Midvale Shopping Center in Madison and Wildwood at the intersection of National Avenue, Cleveland and Highway 100. In January 1961, Schuster's closed its store at Twelfth and Vliet, consolidating the inventory at its Third Street store.

Schuster's had been the dominant retailer in the Milwaukee market for years, with sales ranging in the $40 to $50 million range in the 1950s, but Gimbels was closing the gap. In 1961, Gimbels topped Schuster's volume for the first time when Gimbels' $48 million in sales surpassed Schuster's sales of $47 million.

Profitability is a measure of longevity, and in 1960, Schuster's net profit was $775,000, or 1.7 percent of sales, enough to pay stockholders dividends and fund future expansion. The Gimbels Milwaukee store was equally as profitable, although Gimbels Milwaukee net profits were not reported. Gimbels Milwaukee generated twice the profit that the Gimbels New York store did, according to an article in the *Milwaukee Journal* in 1962. In 1961, Gimbel Brothers had over $422 million in sales, positioning itself as the second-largest retailer in the country behind Federated Department Stores, with $856 million in sales that year.

Schuster's was doing just fine, and it surprised people when, late in 1961, Maurice W. Berger, the head of Gimbels Milwaukee, announced that he was discussing the merging of the two companies with Ralph T. Friedman, chairman of the board for Schuster's. Ed Schuster was in his mid-fifties when he started his store in 1883. After his death in 1904, Albert Friedman replaced him until his death in 1933. Albert's son Max Friedman took over the store and died in 1954. Ralph, Max's brother, must have worried about dying on the job. Ralph Friedman's two sons had no interest in Schuster's, and Ralph was concerned about the lack of a successor. On April 9, 1962, the transaction was completed, with $16 million in Gimbel common stock exchanged for Schuster's stock.

John Mahorka's birthday party in 1961. *Front row, left to right*: Leo Praxel, electrician; Charlie Andrews, chief electrician; unknown; John Mahorka (holding flower), carpenter; Harry Powers, electrician; Christ Schoberth, carpenter foreman. *Back row*: John Salamas, cabinetmaker; unknown; Peter Volkert, electrician. *Courtesy of Harold Badzinski.*

The merger of the two department store chains was the largest retail transfer of ownership in Wisconsin up to that time, with the combined Gimbels-Schusters employing about 4,000 employees in eight stores. The consolidation eliminated the duplicate positions of 175 people, including senior managers, 40 buyers and people in the credit, accounting and publicity departments. All of the hourly people were retained.

In 1962, three unions—the Retail Store Employees, Building Service Employees and Office Employees International Unions—were looking to expand membership by organizing workers in department stores. Unions thought that Gimbels-Schusters' management would have difficulty in merging the workforces of the two department stores. The unions filed for an election about collective bargaining rights at the new Gimbels-Schusters but lost with a vote of 4,117 to 1,311. Management's effort to keep employees happy had paid off. The National Labor Relations Board cleared Gimbels-Schusters of any unfair labor practices. The United States Justice Department filed and then dropped a suit to block the merger, determining that the 57 percent market share of the combined stores was not restraint of trade.

A conscious effort was made to meld the cultures of the two organizations that had so recently been competitors. The tendency at first was for Gimbels people to dominate over the Schuster's people, but after a while, that went away. Two identical dinners, each featuring standing roast beef, were served to over 1,500 employees combined. Department members were seated together and clasped hands across their tables to signify their willingness to work together as a team. The highlight of the evening was "A Ballad of Gimbels and Schusters" sung by the Meridians, a local choral group.

In 1962, Leon Boniface, at the age of forty, came to Gimbels as display manager from the Hecht Company in Washington, D.C. The Gimbels-Schusters merger had just been announced, and one of the first issues Boniface had to deal with was merging the two display department cultures into one. Schuster's culture was more autocratic, while Gimbels' was more laid-back. There were disagreements on the best way to get things done. Direction had to be given with sensitivity toward individual store attitudes.

By the end of 1962, Packard Plaza and Hilldale, the stores planned by Schuster's, were open, and the plans for the Wildwood store were canceled. Basement stores were opened in the Third Street, Mitchell Street and Capital Court stores. Gimbel Brothers finished the year with sales of $462 million and a 2.23 percent net profit.

Schuster's state-of-the-art mainframe computer, printers and punch card readers from the Third Street store were moved to a new data center on the seventh floor. The room had a raised floor for the cables and extra cooling for the heat thrown off by the vacuum tubes. The computer system replaced Gimbels' manual credit authorization system located on the sixth floor, eliminating the need to do a manual look-up in the Dieboldt File System every time a customer wanted to charge his or her purchase.

New competitors were entering the market, including Max and Herb Kohl, who in 1962 opened the first Kohl's Department Store in Brookfield, Wisconsin. The Kohl brothers found that sales in their grocery stores, their primary business, increased by 15 to 20 percent if the grocery store was located near one of their department stores. The Kohl's store targeted mid-range customers, offering a blend of some of the brands that department stores carried and more attractive displays than those that discount stores offered. Checkout stations and more service, but not a salesperson in every department, were features of these new stores. The Kohl brothers started

Bob Heinz, advertising manager; Jane Glasbert, director of public relations; Leon Boniface, display director; and Jim Ostrander with Billie the Brownie. *Courtesy of Milwaukee County Historical Society.*

Charlie Andrews, Harry Badzinski and Frank Manthe. Andrews was the chief electrician and Manthe was maintenance manager. They were celebrating Badzinski's appointment as building superintendent in September 1965. *Courtesy of Harold Badzinski.*

Leo Praxel, electrician, and Chris Schoberth, carpenter, at their retirement party in 1964. *Seated*: Praxel and Schoberth with their wives. *Rear*: Frank Manthe, maintenance and housekeeping manager; Arthur Moore, purchasing agent; Harold Badzinski, store planning. *Courtesy of Harold Badzinski.*

looking for land that they could develop into sites for two new shopping centers, one on the north side and the other on the south side of the Milwaukee market.

Gimbels-Schusters consolidated its selling space to be more efficient. The Third Street store was reduced from five levels to the Basement Store and the first and second floor. Non-selling departments like receiving and marking, traffic and Schuster's wholesale bakery operation, formerly located on South Second Street, were moved to Third Street. All Schuster's corporate functions were moved to Gimbels' downtown store.

PROMOTIONS

In 1960, Maurice Berger, the head of Gimbels-Schusters, started the Fashion Forum as a way to promote Gimbels-Schusters' fashion leadership. A group of seventy-five women who were "active in cultural, civic and club work" from the Milwaukee area were chosen to have lunch and enjoy a fashion show every quarter. The *Milwaukee Scene*, a calendar of local civic and social events and tips on what to wear, was published every three months. It was distributed free to Gimbels-Schusters customers in its stores.

The Fashion Forum presented awards to such notables as Lynn Fontanne, Abigail Van Buren of "Dear Abby" fame and Enid Annenberg Haupt, editor of *Seventeen*. Local recipients of the award included Florence Eiseman, Milwaukee's leading children's fashion designer; and Jack Winter, CEO of Milwaukee's women's pants manufacturer. Mrs. Warren P. Knowles received the award for her efforts in redecorating the governor's mansion.

The annual Fashion Forum Awards Celebration was a significant social event in Milwaukee from 1960 to 1967. Guests and the awardees in formal attire entered at the Plankington Street door and walked down a red carpet to the east bank of elevators. A sixty-foot display featuring the awardee greeted guests in the eighth-floor lobby and served as a backdrop for press photos and TV interviews. Those lucky enough to make the invitation list enjoyed three open bars and were offered a choice of meat or fish and special desserts. Honored guests included the mayor, chief executives of Milwaukee's major corporations and Ben Marcus, one of the organizers of the event.

In 1968, Maurice Berger died unexpectedly, and the Fashion Forum was discontinued. In the mid-1960s, the Eighth Floor Restaurant was renamed the Forum Restaurant after the Fashion Forums.

Fashion shows were used to promote the Gimbels-Schusters brand. The store held up to 150 fashion shows annually as fundraising events for churches, nonprofits and social agencies. The Fashion Forum advisory council selected the nonprofits and churches that received the proceeds from these fashion shows. The display department designed backdrops for fashion shows put on by each store's Teen Board. The 1960 Miss Wisconsin told high school students, "Good grooming implies good citizenship."

In 1963, Boniface worked with the city to create spectacular Christmas decorations over Wisconsin Avenue from the Milwaukee Public Library at Ninth Street to Gimbels-Schusters. The city strung power lines from building to building and created a lighted canopy over Wisconsin Avenue. A Christmas tree, 165 feet high, attached to the

Gimbels-Schusters building completed the effect. The tree had almost three thousand lights and stretched from the store's first-floor canopy to above the roofline. The Christmas tree could be seen from both sides of Wisconsin Avenue and complemented the city's decorations without extending into the pedestrian area. Although the tree broke down into nine sections for easy storage, it was a challenge to put up and take down. The Everbrite Sign Company used radios to communicate with the tall crane and the installer, who stacked the pieces together and secured the structure to the building while suspended in a bosun chair. The famous lighted Christmas tree slowly deteriorated from exposure to Wisconsin's winters and was last used in 1978. There was concern about falling pieces harming pedestrians.

Another Christmas, Boniface hung banners from the sixth-floor windows, but they blew loose because of the fierce winds that roar through the Wisconsin Avenue tunnel. The banners' metal rods were flapping furiously in the wind, threatening the store windows, and the fire department had to be called to secure the wildly flailing objects.

The eighth-floor Forum Restaurant was used to bring in traffic, and Boniface applied his decorating skills to make displays for a week of authentic recipes from restaurants in other cities. Tom Friedman, director of food services, put together authentic dishes from these expensive restaurants but charged modest Gimbels prices. Replicas of the jockey from New York's Club 21 stood on the main floor and in the eighth-floor restaurant to highlight a dish of beef bordelaise—medallions of tenderloin cooked in burgundy wine and shallots. Crystal chandeliers, similar to the ones found at Chasen in Los Angeles, decorated a portion of the Gimbels restaurant where Chicken Alexandria was served. This was chicken simmered in a port wine sauce and served with apples and slivered almonds. A nautical décor enhanced the flounder stuffed with crabmeat, a popular recipe from Bookbinders in Philadelphia.

Boniface used his skills to make the Forum Restaurant a destination for Gimbels-Schusters customers. The restaurant boasted two nude paintings: a woman displayed over the round table where Gimbels executives had lunch together daily and a second of a male that was positioned behind the cash register. A customer complained about the nudity, and Boniface added fig leaves to both paintings.

Ed Danaher, the main-floor aisle manager, was a very dapper dresser, according to Boniface. Danaher, sporting a white carnation in his lapel, would patrol the main floor, making customers feel welcome and assisting women with their strollers and packages. In 1965, Gimbels ran a full-page add in the *Milwaukee Journal* honoring Danaher's completion of sixty years of service. He started as a transfer boy in 1905.

Gimbels-Schusters continued the tradition of holding major sales. Customers flocked to the post-Thanksgiving Holly Days Sale, each receiving a fresh holly sprig. The floral department had an excellent reputation for quality and was in high demand. The department purchased 250 cases of holly to give away at this sale.

In August 1969, 6,200 teenagers flocked to Gimbels-Schuster's "Night of Your Life" event. Local bands The Messengers, Vic Pitts and the Cheaters and Freddie and the Freeloaders played on three stages while the teenagers wrote graffiti on walls and enjoyed a fashion show. Girls in mini dresses called "Chicks in a Cage" danced to the music in cages.

Gimbels-Schusters was a place for people to hang out. The cheerful women's restroom on the second floor had comfortable chairs and was a favorite gathering place for women living on social security. Women would discuss their sewing projects and browse books of dress patterns while sitting around the big cutting tables in the yard goods department.

THE CANDY KITCHEN

The candy kitchen was a Schuster's tradition that Gimbels-Schusters improved upon. In 1968, the candy kitchen, with its four workrooms, was remodeled and doubled in size to supply the needs of the candy departments in eight stores. The kitchen had been making candy that was sold under the name of Char-Mont since 1939. It was located behind the arched windows on the sixth floor of the southwest corner of Gimbels-Schuster's downtown store, producing 550,000 pounds of candy annually.

The greatest poundage was shipped for the Christmas season, but the widest assortment was produced for Easter. Right after Christmas, Allen Crass, the candy kitchen manager, and his staff of thirty-two began producing a wide variety of candies for Easter. Large whipped cream eggs, each molded by hand with twenty different centers, were made from scratch. Center fillings included raspberry, mint, vanilla, butterscotch, maple whipped cream, fruit and nut cream, chocolate fudge, nougat, mint, chocolate and peanut butter meltaway, vanilla, maple, banana, fudge cherry, pineapple, coconut cream, Hawaiian and butter cream.

A story in the *Gimbelite* in 1966 describes the process. Each batch of cream center for the eggs was prepared in one of two huge copper cream beaters. Cooked syrup was poured into the beater, and the temperature was controlled with water that flowed between the beaters' double hulls. The completed batch of cream filling was poured onto a large, flat counter, where Jessie Dombrowski would divide the cream center according to weight and Sue Ann Van Gorder would mold the portions into the shape of an egg.

Martha Kwiecien hand-dipped the cream egg fillings in hot caramel, and Clifford Dolge rolled the eggs in chopped pecans. The centers were then fed onto a conveyor belt leading to an automatic chocolate enrobing machine. The eggs, moving slowly on this belt, were carried over two rotating drums where the bottoms were coated with chocolate and then through a flowing curtain of coating to completely cover the top of the eggs. The eggs were finished with dark chocolate, milk chocolate, caramel, butterscotch, nuts or a pastel frosting called "tropic" and were then aged for four to six weeks before being shipped out to the stores. Some eggs, such as the bonbon eggs, had only a ten-day shelf life.

The kitchen turned out a wide assortment of hand-dipped chocolates, nuts and coconut brittles, bonbons, mint wafers, caramels, chocolate and pecan "Turks," creams, coloate and pecan Annaclairs, fragile chocolate-covered strawberry cordials and more. Tin molds imported from Europe in the late 1930s were used to give the chocolate a higher gloss and a longer shelf life.

TALENTED EXECUTIVES

Being part of the executive tier at Gimbels-Schusters was an exciting career in the 1960s. Carol Larson started as a junior sportswear assistant buyer and became the junior sportswear buyer in the early 1960s. The Gimbel Brothers sportswear buyers traveled regularly as a group, first to London, Paris, Rome and Florence to observe and "absorb" the current fashions and then to Hong Kong and Taiwan to place their orders for the upcoming season. The buying power of the Gimbel Brothers stores allowed the group to meet the minimum quantity the manufacturers required. Larson remembers buying "tons" of fur blend sweaters during the '60s. Gimbel Brothers had an "incredible" buying office, she said. Expertise from Saks

Fifth Avenue was a big help to the New York corporate buying offices in selecting the best vendors.

Larson, a single, professional woman, enjoyed socializing with other buyers over a few drinks at the Swinging Door. Female executives from Gimbels had a favorite table in the Forum Restaurant, and it would always be ready for them when Larson and her co-workers arrived. Larson says she always considered herself to be equal with the male executives, although she took exception with the philosophy that men should be paid more than female executives because they "have to support a family."

Eleanor S. Poss, who became the first female to attain VP level at Gimbels, was one of the executives with whom Larson lunched in the Forum Restaurant. Poss graduated from Vassar and had worked in a social service agency for six years and as the employment supervisor of A.O. Smith's Butler plant before coming to Gimbels in 1945. After working on special assignments for the Gimbels store manager, she was promoted to assistant personnel and training director in 1947. She was promoted to director of personnel in 1960.

Bob Schulz started working in the stockroom right out of high school and returned to Gimbels after he served in the Korean War in 1954. He was promoted to assistant buyer and put in charge of maintaining the unit control records for the furniture inventory, marking off sold items on the control cards and having purchases shipped to the furniture workroom for delivery. He enjoyed meeting and working with the salesmen at all eight stores to fill their orders after the Gimbels-Schusters merger.

Schulz was in charge of setting up periodic furniture warehouse sales held in the Third Street parking ramp, downtown at a building on Plankington or at Mitchell Street. He enjoyed the sales meetings hosted by vendors such as Simmons and Sterns and Foster, with open bars and nice dinners. He tells the story of how an employee from unit control donated her old mattress to be used as a sales tool for a training meeting.

Gimbels was a national company with deep roots in the Milwaukee community. It was attracting the best and the brightest employees and dominating the retail scene. In 1968, Maurice Berger died suddenly, and Leonard C. Hobart was appointed president of the eight-store chain. The company was doing well but would have to deal with another challenge.

MILWAUKEE'S RACE RIOTS

In 1960, 63,000 African Americans lived in a segregated area around the Gimbels-Schusters Third Street store. Before 1962, only a handful of African Americans worked at Gimbels in positions such as maids, cooks or garage attendants. In 1963, Val F. Lindner, the manager representing Gimbels-Schuster's eight Wisconsin stores, told the Wisconsin Industrial Commission that he knew of only 2 African Americans out of their 6,700 employees who held positions higher than sales clerks.

In 1964, Gimbels-Schusters hired two African American North Division seniors as flyers. Gimbels was one of twenty Milwaukee companies that offered fifty African American senior high school students intern positions as part of a program titled Cooperative Training. In the 1965 issues of the *Gimbelite*, the number of African Americans pictured increased. One issue featured a picture of four baseball players, one of whom was African American and worked at Commerce Street. In 1966, Leonard Hobart, who was at that time Gimbels-Schuster's controller, said that more needed to be done to create jobs in the central city.

In the summer of 1967, the racial climate in Milwaukee was tense. On Sunday, July 30, 1967, violence broke out at Third and Center Streets, about four blocks from the Gimbels-Schusters Third Street store. A Woolworth's at Thirteenth and Vliet Streets was looted. Mayor Maier called out the National Guard because of the rioting in an area that ranged from West State Street to Burleigh and First to Fifth Streets.

Jack Koplin, who was in charge of inventory control at the time, went to the store Monday morning and found that the Third Street store's parking garage had been turned into a command post for the Milwaukee Police Department. Waist-high stacks of ammunition were ready to be deployed by the police squads patrolling the area. Koplin walked into the building to assess the damage but was warned by a policeman that two snipers were in the vicinity. The display island windows on the east side of the store were smashed and the merchandise had been taken, but the store itself escaped unscathed. For two hundred days, starting in August 1967, James Groppi led a fair housing march demonstrating for jobs and better housing.

Sales in the Third Street store declined after the riots because, as Bob Schultz remembers, there was a lot of tension. Gimbels-Schusters kept Third Street open for four years but in August 1971, "The Colossus of Third Street" closed.

Gimbels Third Street in the 1970s after closing. *Courtesy of Jack Koplin.*

The Gimbels Third Street building today. In 1984, the building was sheathed and stucco was used to seal the first floor. *Courtesy of Paul Geenen.*

In 1967, while driving to Madison to view a site for the new East Town store, Koplin told Bruce Gimbel that he thought Capital Court sales would soon be affected by white flight from Milwaukee's central city neighborhoods.

Max and Herb Kohl, who had shown their skill in site selection by growing their company from a single grocery store into a sixty-plus-store chain, were buying up property in Brown Deer and Greendale for two new shopping centers. Charlie Zadok was working in Gimbel Brothers' New York offices on plans for four new branch stores: two for the Kohl brothers' new shopping centers and one each in Appleton and Madison. Zadok contracted the design work to outside firms because of the large number of stores that were being planned at all four Gimbel Brothers divisions.

Store hours were being extended along with convenient suburban locations. On August 10, 1969, Gimbels-Schusters opened on Sundays to accommodate the increased number of working wives. Gimbels-Schusters paid its employees time and a half for working Sundays and had no difficulty in staffing its stores.

Gimbels management had successfully navigated through some difficult shoals—incorporating the staff of Schuster's into the new organization, opening two new stores and dealing with the death of a key executive. People were moving to the suburbs, and Gimbels was poised to take advantage of that trend.

TIMELINE

1961	Schuster's open its Packard Plaza store
1961	Schuster's closes its store at Twelfth and Vliet
April 9, 1962	The Gimbels-Schusters merger is completed
October 25, 1962	Gimbels-Schusters opens its Hilldale store
1962	Max Kohl opens the first Kohl's Department Store

1963	Gimbels-Schusters adds the Basement Store to Capital Court
1965	Gimbels-Schusters reduces the selling floors of its Third Street store
September 29, 1966	Bernard Gimbel dies
1966	Ralph Friedman dies
July 25, 1968	Maurice Berger dies, and Leonard Hobart succeeds him as president of the Gimbels Wisconsin Stores Division
August 10, 1969	Gimbels opens on Sundays
August 22, 1970	The Gimbels Third Street store closes

CHAPTER 8

BATUS Purchases Gimbel Brothers

1970–1980

EXPANSION

Baby boomers were shopping! This was a decade of rapid store expansion and strong sales growth. Gimbel Brothers was building anchor stores in major shopping centers in New York, Pittsburgh, Philadelphia and Milwaukee. This investment would put Gimbel Brothers on the big stage and would force equally big changes in its leadership.

In March 1971, Gimbels opened its Appleton store, the first branch that it built outside of the Milwaukee market area. Aid Association for Lutherans (AAL) financed construction of the new store with a generous lease package. Some of Appleton's oldest buildings, including Geenen's Dry Goods, were torn down to create the site. AAL headquarters were located just down the street from Gimbels' new store. Gimbels saw Appleton as being located in the geographic center of an area between Green Bay and Fond du Lac, with a heavy concentration of upper-income customers.

In the fall of 1971, Gimbels opened two new branch stores, Southridge and East Town, and a year later, in August 1972, its Northridge store opened. Gimbels was a major player in the Milwaukee, Madison and Appleton markets.

This expansion had a price. By 1973, Gimbels stock had dropped to less than half of its high of $47.50 and had become a target for acquisition. In August 1973, Brown & Williamson purchased Gimbels for $23.00 a share, at a total cost of approximately $200 million. Gimbel Brothers became part of the retailing group that included stores in Germany, Britain, Brazil and the United States. Brown & Williamson's plan was to dominate the retail world the same way it dominated tobacco. It named this retail group BATUS (British American Tobacco U.S.).

CHANGES IN THE MANAGEMENT TEAM

On March 18, 1975, Richard G. Shapiro became corporate president of Gimbel Brothers. Bruce Gimbel had spent almost a year looking for the right person to take over the company. Shapiro, only forty-nine, came from Filene's in Boston and Lord & Taylor in New York. Bruce Gimbel thought that the company needed a young manager and promised to give Shapiro "a very free hand to operate."

Gimbel Brothers was not doing well. The New York store had taken a $6 million hit on bad charge accounts and was building an expensive new store on Eighty-sixth Street, on New York's pricy East Side. Gimbels Wisconsin was facing strong competition from Sears and JCPenney in Milwaukee, total retail selling space in Madison had doubled in size and its Appleton store was losing money.

Bruce Gimbel retired on August 31, 1975. The tradition of Gimbel family members managing the company had come to an end, and the articles of the time talked about the need for more professional management. Dayton's in Minneapolis and Federated Department Stores were the last two major retail chains where family members were still involved.

While this was happening, Leonard Hobart and Alan Sunshine were managing Gimbels in Wisconsin. Hobart had started at Gimbels in 1936 and had almost forty years of experience. He used his skills with numbers for long-range planning and saw himself as "the dreamer," the one who was responsible for planning Gimbels' future. Between 1971 and 1972, he orchestrated the opening of four branch stores: Hilldale, Appleton, Southridge and Northridge.

Sunshine came from Gimbels Philadelphia in 1973 to become the fashion merchandise manager at the Milwaukee division. In 1974, he was made president and was responsible for all sales promotions. Department store experts saw a two-member management team as being the best practice for running a company the size of Gimbels Midwest.

Jack Koplin and Leonard Hobart at Koplin's twenty-fifth celebration in 1977. *Courtesy of Jack Koplin.*

Hobart believed his role included working to build a better community. He served as president of the Citizen's Governmental Research Bureau and vice-president of the Milwaukee Association of Commerce. He also served on the boards of the Florentine Opera, Summerfest and the Downtown Development.

Hobart also initiated small but important efforts to increase diversity in Gimbels employees. In 1970, Gimbels hired more than thirty African American employees to work in five branch stores. Gimbels was one of thirty-four Milwaukee employers that participated in a JOBS (National Alliance of Businessmen's Job Opportunities in the Business Sector) program with a goal to hire over four thousand unemployed African American and Hispanic workers. Federal JOBS program funds paid for basic skills training of these workers. The 1975 photos in the *Gimbelite* show a small but noticeable increase in the number of African American employees at Gimbels, an indicator that efforts to add diversity to Gimbels' workforce were beginning to have an impact.

Sometime in 1975, Martin Kramer became chairman of Gimbel Brothers, and Allen Johnson continued as chairman of Saks Fifth Avenue. Richard Shapiro left the company once Kramer came on board. Kramer had come from Gimbels Pittsburgh and prior to that had served as president of Maas Brothers in Tampa, Florida. His aggressive style would be a big change from the hands-off, relaxed style of Bruce Gimbel.

In 1975, Kramer recruited Burnett W. Donoho, an executive who had worked for Kramer as chief operating officer at Maas Brothers. Donoho, who had a reputation as someone who always made his numbers, replaced

Eleanor Poss, who was retiring, as vice-president of personnel. Donoho's personable style was put to good use quickly. In 1976, the Retail Clerks Union attempted to organize the hourly employees at Gimbels' Mitchell Street store. Donoho visited the store often, was well liked and was effective in talking to the employees about the advantages of not joining the union. Donoho, working with Bud Schneider, the store manager, won a decisive election, with 61 percent of the employees voting not to join the union.

On June 31, 1976, Hobart retired, Sunshine was appointed CEO of Gimbels Midwest and Donoho became executive vice-president. Sunshine was responsible for sales, while Donoho managed personnel, finance and operations. The Sunshine-Donoho team was now running Gimbels Midwest.

Sunshine was active in the community. He served on the boards of the Milwaukee Symphony Orchestra, the Greater Milwaukee Committee and the Mount Sinai Medical Center. He helped raise funds for the United Fund, the Milwaukee Art Center and the Channel 10 Auction. Mayor Henry Maier appointed him to lead the new Milwaukee River Technical task force that was studying better uses for the Milwaukee River.

In June 1978, Alan Sunshine resigned to become president of a Kansas City clothing chain. Kramer appointed Thomas G. Grimes from Gimbels as chairman of the board of Gimbels. Grimes's last position had been vice-president and general merchandise manager at the Gimbels New York store.

Kramer described Grimes as being soft-spoken, with a great sense of humor and "a twinkle in his eye." Donoho was promoted to president and chief operating officer of Gimbels. Grimes was responsible for merchandising and sales promotion, while Donoho was responsible for administration, personnel, finance and operations. The Grimes-Donoho team was now running Gimbels Midwest.

Kramer felt that Gimbels Midwest stores had to be more "theatrical" and gave Grimes the money to remodel the Gimbels stores. Grimes changed the merchandise mix to attract a younger and more sophisticated customer. Updated stores, special events and new brands that appealed to young customers were designed to make the Gimbels stores fun places to shop.

Grimes embarked on a $40 million program to remodel the Mayfair, Southridge, Northridge and Hilldale stores. The stores' selling floors were redesigned with shallow, racetrack-style aisles that featured expanded fashion departments such as junior sportswear. The stores looked dated; in fact, the joke was that the Tasty Town restaurant in the Northridge store should be curtained off and then reopened, as its '50s décor had come back and was again popular.

Donoho used his skills at controlling costs to make Gimbels profitable. Managers learned not to come in with high preliminary budgets just to make it easy to show budget cuts. He tightly controlled the cost of salespeople, as this was one of Gimbels Midwest's largest expenses. He told Mike Hammack in personnel that employees would be offered a certain new benefit when "Lake Michigan freezes over." When Lake Michigan did freeze over one winter, Donoho told Hammack to "start walking." Donoho was from Kentucky and liked to share pithy sayings. One of his favorites was "that dog won't hunt," which was used, for example, when Donoho turned down a manager's request for a budget increase.

The merchandise and the décor were not the only things that Kramer felt needed changing. Kramer thought that Gimbels was old-fashioned and brought in Stanley Butterfield as director of stores. Butterfield brought in his own store managers. He would visit a branch store, suggest merchandising changes and then return to the store the following Friday afternoon. If the changes had not been implemented satisfactorily, the store manager was fired on the spot. Butterfield replaced all but three of the ten store managers. The story goes that Tony Cusatis, the Appleton store manager, had spoken with Leon Boniface, display manager, before Butterfield's visit, and he warned Cusatis to make the required changes before Butterfield returned. When Butterfield returned, Cusatis's sales managers were standing at attention in front of their areas of responsibility, ready for Butterfield's review. Cusatis kept his job.

There was a natural tension at Gimbels between the people involved in managing the stores and those responsible for purchasing the merchandise that was sold in the stores. Store managers' primary focus was on sales and expenses, while people in merchandising focused on sales and the difference between the cost of the merchandise and the selling price (gross margin). Store managers' focus was on selling as much as they could at the lowest cost. This tension could be seen when, for example, the merchandising staff would provide training opportunities for the salespeople but get resistance from the stores about the expense of taking salespeople off the selling floor. Added to this natural tension, Kramer created a new level of tension that ran between management at Gimbels Midwest and Gimbel Brothers.

Kramer appointed Steve Westerfield vice-president and corporate director of all Gimbels stores. The tension now crisscrossed randomly between the merchants, the store managers, Gimbels Midwest and Gimbel Brothers. Gimbels Midwest called in outside management consultants to improve communication. Kramer tried to reinforce the message that senior managers were responsible for their own stores in a meeting of all three divisions at corporate headquarters in New York.

Long hours were expected from executives. Butterfield told a store manager that "you can't take extra vacations" after the store manager took a week away from the store to fulfill his responsibilities with the Wisconsin National Guard. Grimes always worked Saturday mornings, and it was an unwritten rule that buyers and divisional merchandise managers would also. Executives working on Saturday mornings dropped in at the employee cafeteria to make sure that they were seen. Often, work took priority over family. The hardlines merchandise manager told a divisional merchandise manager that his wife understood the need to work Saturday mornings. Executives cleared out of the building two minutes after Grimes left the store on Saturdays at noon.

In 1979, Robert Suslow replaced Kramer as president and chief executive officer of Saks and Gimbels, and William Rush replaced Butterfield as director of stores. Rush, who came from Gimbels Pittsburgh, showed a new level of empathy toward his store managers and started to knit things back together.

Gimbels had an effective training program for recent college graduates. Management trainees attended formal classes for eight days, with a store manager, a divisional merchandise manager and the visual merchandise director talking about their areas of responsibilities and answering questions. The class visited a store, where they were divided into teams and each assigned an area. Each team rearranged, colorized and sized the merchandise and then made a presentation to the class. After several months of on-the-job training, the management trainees were assigned to buyers and store managers.

Gimbels advertised that it was the "Store with More," a full-service department store that offered fashions appealing to a wide age range of women. Yard goods, notions and garden shop were dropped at all stores. Some stores eliminated their food, appliance and toy departments. Housewares was renamed Habitat and was decorated with natural materials to dramatize the trendy imports purchased by the buyers in overseas markets.

The sales of the new, higher-margin fashion merchandise did not completely offset sales lost from the discontinued departments. In fact, some of the old selling space was now being used to store fixtures. Grimes set up sale committees, and store managers took turns negotiating the major promotions with the divisional merchandising managers. This was tried for Spring Fling and Anniversary Sale and was so successful that the format was extended to six major sales held each year. Bonus items only available on the first day of the sale were used to create a sense of urgency.

Employees

All the tension and pressure at the management level was not transferred to the salespeople. Gimbels continued to be a good place to work for them, and turnover among the full-time salespeople was low. The company-sponsored bowling teams, department Christmas parties and summer picnics were long gone. But the lavish dinners for long-term employees continued. In 1975, prime rib was served to over two thousand people at two events. Eleanor Poss, who was retiring as vice-president of personnel and was the first female senior executive at Gimbels, hosted one last time before retiring after her twenty-nine years of service. The ten- and twenty-five-year clubs met every year and continued building a sense of loyalty and teamwork. A generous lifetime 20 percent discount often brought twenty-five-year club members back to the store to shop.

Socializing among the Gimbels executives was done on a more informal basis than in years past. Managers liked to meet after hours at Sal's, which is now closed, and the Swinging Door, a very smoky bar located at 219 East Michigan Street. The Swinging Door opened the day after Prohibition ended in 1933 and has been a popular place for downtown workers to meet ever since. Grimes sometimes would pick up the bar tab for Gimbels managers.

Grimes liked a surprise. For example, he made up an excuse for the store managers to meet and instead took them out on Lake Michigan on the *Iroquois* party boat. Phil Johnson, when he was vice-president of personnel, hosted backyard barbeques at his home for a few of the store managers, personnel managers and wives. One memorable party was a three-county scavenger hunt.

Gimbels was in a good position to compete. Gimbels branch stores were being remodeled, and the merchandise was being updated. Grimes had developed a format for compelling promotions that were ringing up sales at record levels. Rush, the new director of stores, was building a new management team. Donoho was controlling expenses, and the Gimbels Midwest division was profitable. *Retail Week* named Robert Suslow the Man of the Year in its December 15, 1979 edition. It looked like Suslow was going to be able to turn Gimbel Brothers around.

A 1970 Gimbels employee party celebrating America's landing on the moon. *Courtesy of Jack Koplin.*

Ella Linde and Jack Koplin at Ella's retirement party in 1975. Linde holds the service record, working for Gimbels for sixty-eight years. Her mother told her that Gimbels was a good place to work. Linde worked for Koplin in accounts payable. *Courtesy of Jack Koplin.*

Milwaukee's Beloved Department Stores

TIMELINE

March 11, 1971	Gimbels Appleton
August 12, 1971	Gimbels closes its Third Street store
Autumn 1971	Gimbels Southridge opens
October 14, 1971	Gimbels East Town opens
August 1972	Southgate Mall is enclosed
August 2, 1972	Gimbels Northridge opens
August 1, 1973	Brown & Williamson purchases Gimbel Brothers
March 1974	Alan Sunshine becomes president of Gimbels
March 18, 1975	Richard Shapiro becomes Gimbel Brothers' corporate president
August 31, 1975	Bruce Gimbel retires from Gimbel Brothers
1975	Martin Kramer becomes chairman of Gimbel Brothers and Allen R. Johnson continues as chairman of Saks
December 1975	Burnett Donoho joins Gimbels Milwaukee as vice-president of personnel
June 31, 1976	Leonard Hobart retires
January 1977	Alan Sunshine becomes CEO of Gimbels
1978	Mayfair and Northridge are renovated

April 1978	Tom Grimes comes to Gimbels
June 29, 1978	Alan Sunshine resigns to become president of a Woolf Brothers, a Kansas City–based clothing store chain
June 29, 1978	Tom Grimes becomes chairman of Gimbels Midwest
1978	Burnett Donoho becomes president and chief operating officer
1979	Robert Suslow is appointed president and chief executive officer of Saks and Gimbels
1979	William Rush replaces Stanley Butterfield as director of stores
October 7, 1980	Bruce Gimbel dies

CHAPTER 9

The Changing of the Guard

1980–2000

DOWNTOWN REMODELING

In 1980, the financial world was struggling with expensive oil prices, high interest rates and rapid changes. Traditional financial barriers between countries were falling, and formerly staid institutions such as banks were investing in international high-risk investments, where they could earn much greater profits than they could from their depositors. Hostile purchases were used to acquire sick companies and generate lucrative transaction fees for investors. The weak firms' assets were then sold off and the infrastructure consolidated to pay for the acquisition.

In 1980, Gimbel Brothers was coming out of a decade of turmoil, with its New York and Pittsburgh divisions still struggling. Gimbels Midwest, however, was the number-one shopping destination for over half of the women in the Milwaukee market. Every three or four months, Gimbels chairman Tom Grimes was announcing over the PA system of the downtown store that Gimbels Midwest had broken another major sales record. Customers were flocking to its newly updated branch stores. Gimbels Midwest was the dominant retailer in the Wisconsin market and could compete with anyone.

From 1981 to 1983, the downtown store was remodeled at a cost of $50 million, more than the combined cost of remodeling all the branch stores. Tasty Town was closed and the food departments moved to free up prime first-floor selling space. The second floor was connected to the three planned

Marketplace logo. *Courtesy of Paul Geenen.*

all-weather skywalks: the Plankington Mall to the west, the Riverside Theater to the north and the bank across the river to the east.

In October 1981, the Marketplace opened in the lower level of an area formerly occupied by the Basement Store. The finest delicatessens in New York had been studied for food ideas. The bakery, delicatessen and wine departments offered gourmet treats such as pâté, caviar and freshly baked croissants. Natural wood fixtures displayed a wide selection of preserves, wine vinegars and mustards. Customers could browse Plexiglas displays of freshly roasted coffee and bulk teas. The salespeople were trained to help customers select the proper California premium wine for their evening dinner.

Customers selected their own flowers from those displayed behind the glass wall of the floral department's walk-in cooler. A wide selection of cookbooks and coordinated party goods was displayed on custom-designed Hallmark fixtures. The earth-tone floor was made of Italian tile and gave customers the feeling of a Mediterranean kitchen. The Marketplace was a bold statement to attract younger, more affluent customers.

On August 26, 1982, almost a year after Gimbels Marketplace opened, Milwaukee's Grand Avenue Mall directly west of Gimbels was completed at a cost of $60 million. Mayor Henry Maier, the head of the Department of City Development, real estate executives and Gimbels executives proudly cut the ribbon in the dramatic multilevel central arcade. This was a bold melding of the old and new, connecting two anchor department stores—

Gimbels and Boston Store—with the historic Plankington arcade and the new shopping concourse. The opening was a great success. The traffic in the Grand Avenue Mall was so dense that the Mrs. Fields cookie store in the second floor of the Plankington Mall became the highest-volume store of its franchise. People lined up waiting to be seated in the Gimbels Bridge restaurant on the skywalk connecting to the Grand Avenue Mall.

EMPLOYEES

Early in the 1980s, Gimbels was still a fun place to work for many, and most were staying. The ten- and twenty-five-year clubs had 770 members, with 22 working at Gimbels for more than fifty years and 2 having completed sixty-five years of service.

Bill Rush's birthday party. *Left to right, first row*: Linda Higgens, Bob Swanson, Marti Kemp, Judy Householder, Louise Davison; *standing*: Bill Reid; *third row*: Stan Sapiro, Jerry Litton, Ed Manning, Chuck Giovetti, Bud Schneider, John Spahn, Tom Grimes, Gary Guetzow, Dave Lazovik, Bill Rush, Roy Boutillier. *Courtesy of Bud Schneider.*

Staff from the Packard Plaza store on the *Iroquois*. *Courtesy of Bud Schneider.*

Gimbelites liked to socialize. Bill Rush, the director of stores, invited some of the store managers and divisional merchandise managers to his backyard for a birthday celebration. Employees from the Packard Plaza store took an excursion on the *Iroquois* one early spring day.

In 1981, a survey of hourly and line supervisors found that employees were getting along with their co-workers, understood their responsibilities and thought their supervisors were doing a good job. The survey found, however, that communication and training needed to be improved.

African Americans and Hispanics were being hired mostly for jobs behind the scenes, such as at the Third Street warehouse. Minorities did not see Gimbels as a good place to work. They were more often exposed to the sexual harassment that was common in retailing and resigned even as new minorities were hired. One former Gimbels executive recalled that it was unusual in the 1980s for a woman to report a sexual harassment incident because doing so was "the kiss of death." In isolated cases, store executives involved in such incidents were either terminated or severely reprimanded, but none was prosecuted.

THE END

In the early 1980s, consumers were looking for more shopping choices while at the same time the rapid advancements in information systems made it possible for retailers to identify more clearly the demographics of their customers. Big box stores like Target were offering a wide assortment of attractively designed and low-cost merchandise. Category-killer stores were opening in large strip centers, dominating classifications such as electronics or toys and forcing department stores out of these businesses. Kohl's Department Stores applied the racetrack pattern used by department stores to its single-floor design, allowing shoppers to find what they want quickly. BATUS's answer to this competition was Thimbles, a store that featured moderately priced classic fashions appealing to career women. BATUS opened Thimbles stores for a short time in both the Northridge and Southridge malls. Retailers would pay a high price for bad decisions during this time of rapidly changing customer shopping habits.

In June 1982, BATUS purchased Marshall Field's. In the Milwaukee market, BATUS now owned Kohl's Grocery Stores, Kohl's Department Stores and Gimbels, in addition to the newly acquired Marshall Field's store at Mayfair Mall. BATUS's large number of retail outlets in the Milwaukee market caused the FCC to demand that BATUS sell some stores. In 1984, both the Mitchell Street and Capital Court Gimbels stores closed. Southside customers would no longer be able to purchase a Polish prune spread called *powidla* at the Mitchell Street deli. On the last day, Bud Schneider, the Mitchell Street store manager, walked through the store, thanked his employees and gave each associate a corsage. All employees at both stores were placed in new jobs at other stores.

In 1985, Sir James Goldsmith and his investor group offered a hostile bid of $21.7 billion for BATUS. Goldsmith was a British media magnate who had already made millions as a corporate raider in the U.S. market. He had dual citizenship in Britain and France and was a maverick financier who, according to his obituary, lived a life without borders. He had five homes and a net worth of almost $2 billion.

In 1985, Gimbels Midwest had sales of $195 million and before-tax profits of $12 million, but it was the only division of the three Gimbel Brothers divisions to make a profit. In its annual report, BATUS described the offsetting $12 million loss of the other two divisions as "extremely disappointing."

BATUS announced on January 13, 1986, that Marshall Field's, Gimbel Brothers and Kohl's Grocery and Department Stores would be sold. The

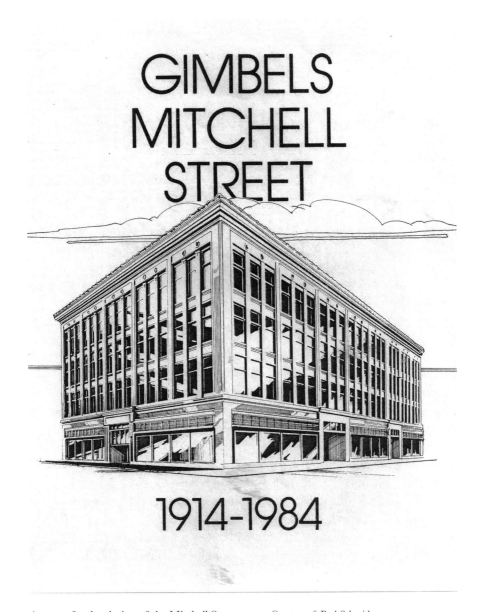

A poster for the closing of the Mitchell Street store. *Courtesy of Bud Schneider.*

Florence Gillett and Jack Koplin with sales checks from the $10 million Bonus Day in the Anniversary Sale of October 1985. *Courtesy of Jack Koplin.*

reason given was the poor performance of Gimbel Brothers, but the underlying cause was as a defense against Goldsmith's hostile takeover. Gimbel Brothers real estate, particularly its New York store, which covered an entire block, was worth more than the company was as a going concern. The three chains—Marshall Field's, Gimbels and Kohl's—had a total of 25,500 employees and combined sales of $1.36 billion. BATUS hoped that the three Gimbel Brothers divisions could be sold as a going concern.

The announcement by BATUS that it was putting the company up for sale probably was a surprise to Gimbels Midwest management since a Gimbels spokesperson had bragged in late 1985 that Gimbels Midwest would see its biggest year in 1986. In fact, on the first day of its Anniversary Sale in October 1985, Gimbels Midwest had its biggest Bonus Day ever, ringing up $10 million in sales. This announcement of the sale of Gimbels Midwest also took the entire Milwaukee community by surprise.

Early in 1985, Burnett Donoho, president and CFO of Gimbels Midwest, had moved to Marshall Field's as its president and CFO. This was a promotion for Donoho because of the larger size of the Fields organization. When

BATUS put Marshall Field's up for sale, Phillip B. Miller, the chairman and CEO of Marshall Field's, and Donoho offered a $900 million management buyout of both the Marshall Field's stores and the four largest Gimbels stores. However, BATUS accepted Dayton-Hudson's higher offer of $1.04 billion. The Grand Avenue, Northridge, Southridge and Hilldale stores would become Marshall Field's stores owned by Dayton-Hudson, while the rest of the Gimbels stores would close.

Gimbels' Going-Out-of-Business Sale began on May 16 and ended on August 16, 1986. The closing date was 144 years after Adam Gimbel opened his "Palace of Trade" in Vincennes, 102 years after Ed Schuster opened his store on Twelfth and Walnut and 99 years after Adam opened his new dry goods store on the corner of Plankington and Wisconsin.

On a rainy Saturday, August 16, 1986, Gimbels said goodbye to its customers in a newspaper ad: "It has been our privilege to serve you…for almost 100 years." Newspapers ran articles recognizing Gimbels' longtime employees who were members of the twenty-five- and fifty-year clubs. The downtown store looked very sad and raggedy in its final days. The signs declaring "The End Is Near" leaning askew in the windows completed the dismal feeling.

More than seven thousand employees lost their jobs when Gimbels closed. The city lost the charitable contributions and advertising revenues, and local suppliers lost a significant customer. Customers mourned, "Oh, I just loved Gimbels." It was a good place to work and a good place to shop.

After Gimbels' Going-Out-of-Business Sale, Marshall Field's, now owned by Dayton-Hudson, temporarily closed the Grand Avenue, Northridge, Southridge and Hilldale Gimbels stores. Marshall Field's completed limited renovations and re-merchandised the stores with its own stock. In October 1986, Marshall Field's reopened the Grand Avenue store, with Mayor Henry Maier and many Marshall Field's executives attending. There were no customers rushing through the door after the ribbon was cut, but the familiar Gimbels salespeople, now Marshall Field's employees, were standing behind the counters, ready to take care of their new Field's customers.

In 1986, Bill Kellogg, chairman of Kohl's Department Stores, completed a management buyout of the thirty-nine Kohl's stores. He partnered with the Suslow investment firm, BATUS and Simon Group, a developer of shopping centers. Suslow was the former CEO of Gimbel Brothers and Saks, and the Simon Group saw a potential for new occupants for its shopping centers. At this time, Kohl's Department Stores was doing about $150 million in sales and would get many of the brands formerly carried at Gimbels. Kellogg was

The "I Survived the Final Chapter but Gimbels Didn't" group. *Front, left to right*: Bill Mallonee, Jack Koplin, Ralph Wenning, unknown; *rear*: Fred Wade, Harvey Brunsch, unknown, unknown, Dick Tyler, unknown, unknown, Paul ?, Greg Fitting, unknown, unknown, unknown, Dorothy ?. *Courtesy of Jack Koplin.*

Bud –
Remembering all the
good times...
Thanks for your ongoing
support. our team was
the Best!
Bill

Bill Rush's thank-you note to Bud Schneider. *Courtesy of Bud Schneider.*

well liked by Kohl's Department Store employees, who felt that their future was in good hands.

In 1990, Marshall Field's announced an ambitious $40 million renovation plan for the former Gimbels stores to maintain its market share in the face of new competition from H.C. Prange Company. Prange, headquartered in Green Bay, had stores in smaller Wisconsin markets and sorely wanted to enter the Milwaukee market. In a sudden reversal, in June of the same year, Dayton-Hudson canceled plans for the $40 million renovation of the Grand Avenue and branch stores. Instead, Dayton-Hudson put the downtown store building up for sale.

Customers expected to find in the Grand Avenue, Northridge and Southridge stores upscale merchandise similar to what Marshall Field's was selling in stores such as Mayfair in Milwaukee or Old Orchard in Chicago. Instead, customers found moderate price range merchandise in stores that looked identical to the old Gimbels stores except for the new signs over the doors. Customers looking for upscale merchandise were disappointed and drifted away.

In 1997, Marshall Field's closed its stores at Grand Avenue, Northridge and Southridge. At the Northridge Mall, the closing of Marshall Field's, Younkers and JCPenney ended the operating covenant that the mall's smaller stores were under. The small stores soon started leaving, and Northridge shopping mall became another casualty of Gimbels' demise.

In 1998, after lengthy negotiations, Bill Orenstein, CEO of Williams Development Corporation, completed the purchase of the downtown Gimbel building for $3 million. Dayton-Hudson had the building on its books at $20 million, but Orenstein pointed out that the building needed work and had costly hidden problems.

Renovation of the old Gimbels downtown building started near the end of 1999. Since the block-long building is really six buildings put up at different times, major modifications were required to reuse the space. The four corners of the building had been built first, and the middle section facing the river and Plankington were filled in later. Williams Development tore down the center section facing Plankinton to create a courtyard for the Residence Inn by Marriott. The building's footprint now looked like a wide, inverted horseshoe. The four stories that Williams Development removed dated to 1919 and had been sided with corrugated metal. Once the building was gone the developer found that the marshy ground would not support the circular drive for the hotel entrance, and more than 120 pilings were driven into the soil to stabilize it. The total cost of renovating the building came to almost $60 million. The Art Moderne style of the building, with its rare white terra cotta exterior, earned it a designation as a national historic site. This designation generated important tax credits that made redeveloping the building financially possible.

Today, the building is managed as a commercial condominium, with a Residence Inn by Marriott and ASQ (American Society for Quality) owning their own space and Williams Development Corporation owning the remaining space of retail, office and parking areas. The basement space, where the Marketplace was, is now an underground parking garage, and the Westinghouse escalators from the 1936 World's Fair were scrapped.

This was not an easy or simple project, as the ASQ headquarters, Marriott Hotel and Williams Development space each had their own unique requirements for access and privacy. More than two-thirds of the building is now used for common areas to provide for entrances, elevators and corridors. The top floor of the building that ASQ purchased on the corner of Plankington and Michigan was removed to emphasize the clean lines of the structure.

The building on the corner that Jacob Gimbel first surveyed in 1886 and where Adam Gimbel opened his dry goods store a year later is still in use. It has survived a depression, two world wars and immense changes in the country's financial structure. Gimbels employees had been watching the store every business day for almost one hundred years, making sure it was an inviting place for Milwaukee customers to shop. Today, a new group of workers offers marketing, data services and hospitality to customers from around the world.

The building's location on the RiverWalk makes it an appealing place for both pedestrians and businesses. The walk started over thirty-five years ago by Gimbels today runs for almost two miles from Humboldt Avenue to Milwaukee's harbor. This public-private development stimulated the construction of new condos, apartments, restaurants and the corporate headquarters of both Manpower and ASQ that line its path.

Many of the people who made Gimbels the dominant player in Milwaukee's retail market have new careers. People moved on and, with lessons learned, created new, exciting careers that were previously unimagined.

The signs of Gimbels' presence have disappeared for the most part. On December 20, 2011, the original Gimbels store in downtown Vincennes, Indiana, was destroyed by fire. The letters of the "Planet Fitness" sign seem to be small compared to the bulk of the white terra cotta building in downtown Milwaukee. One misses the bigger-than-life "Gimbels" that boldly proclaimed its presence.

A reunion T-shirt. *Courtesy of Bud Schneider.*

A certain feeling of sadness lingers, not just for the employees but also for the customers, who still say, "I miss Gimbels!" Many Gimbels and Schuster's employees felt they were part of a family and made friendships that continued on after the store closed. Schuster's Leisure Club met at the Crystal Palace on National Avenue for years, and its two hundred members each paid six-dollar annual dues. Drop-in Gimbelites are welcome at Petra's Restaurant at 1657 South 108th Street in Milwaukee at noon on the second Wednesday of every month.

On July 19, 1990, Gimbels and Schuster's employees planned a reunion as part of Festa Italiana, one of Milwaukee's popular ethnic festivals. It was raining so hard that the program had to be canceled due to the danger of electrocution by the sound equipment. More than three hundred people, arranged by branch store, paraded from Plankington and Wisconsin to the Summerfest grounds. People from Gimbels' display department resurrected the original Billie the Brownie float for the parade. Later, after the weather cleared, people met at the Gimbels memorabilia tent on the Festa Italiana grounds to drink beer and reminisce.

In 1986, before Gimbels closed, employees requested one last history of the company, but Irene Baer, editor of Gimbels' employee publications for many years, wrote in the final issue of *Front and Forward* that she found it too painful to write that history. I hope that this last request has now been honored.

TIMELINE

November 8, 1981	Gimbels opens Marketplace
1981	BATUS opens Thimbles stores in Northridge and Southridge
June 11, 1982	BATUS acquires Marshall Field's
August 26, 1982	Grand Avenue Mall opens
Spring of 1983	Hilldale is remodeled
1984	Gimbels sheaths the Third Street warehouse
August 18, 1984	The Mitchell Street store closes
Early 1985	Burnett Donoho becomes Marshall Field's president and COO
Spring of 1985	RiverWalk segment in front of Gimbels is finished
October 1985	Gimbels' single largest sales day is attained on Bonus Day
1985	Jamie Goldsmith puts together a hostile takeover of BATUS
January 13, 1986	BATUS announces the sale of Gimbel Brothers

May 16, 1986	Gimbels' Going-Out-of-Business Sale starts
August 16, 1986	Gimbels closes
June 1986	BATUS accepts Dayton-Hudson offer for Marshall Fields
October 1986	Marshall Field's reopens four Gimbels stores as Field's stores
July 17, 1990	Gimbels employees hold reunion
1997	Marshall Field's closes three of the four former Gimbels stores
1998	Williams Development Corporation buys Gimbels' Grand Avenue store
1999	Visit Milwaukee becomes the first tenant in the redeveloped Gimbels building
2004	Target (Dayton-Hudson) sells Marshall Field's to May Company
February 2005	Federated Department Stores (Macy's) buys May Company

Bibliography

Gurda, John. *The Making of Milwaukee*. N.p.: Milwaukee County Historical Society, 1999.

Hine, Tomas. *I Want That! How We All Became Shoppers*. New York: HarperCollins, 2002.

Kynaston, David. *The Financial Times: A Centenary History*. New York: Penguin Books Ltd., 1988.

Milwaukee County Historical Society. *Gimbel Brothers, 1840–1986*. Manuscript collection.

Milwaukee Public Library, Humanities, Milwaukee History Clipping Index, 1970–1990.

Polacheck, Hilda Scott. *I Came as a Stranger: The Story of a Hull House Girl*. Champaign: University of Illinois Press, 1989.

Schmidt, Lois. *Milwaukee Journal*, April 17, 1994.

Schultz, Stanley. *The Great Depression: A Primary Source History*. Milwaukee: Gareth Stevens, 2006.

Soucek, Gayle. *Marshall Field's: The Store that Helped Build Chicago*. Charleston, SC: The History Press, 2010.

About the Author

Paul Geenen is a retired entrepreneur, an author and a grandfather of eight. He wrote *Milwaukee's Bronzeville: 1900–1950*, a history of African Americans in Milwaukee that was published by Arcadia Publishing in 2006.

Geenen graduated from the University of Wisconsin and worked for Dayton's in Minneapolis, Circuit City in Richmond, Virginia, Gold Triangle in Miami, Florida, and Gimbels in Milwaukee. He joined Gimbels in 1976 as a buyer and was divisional merchandise manager of the Marketplace when he left in 1983. For the next seven years, he worked in sales, first at Computers Unlimited in Milwaukee and then Innovative Computer Products in Indianapolis.

He and his partner started Galaxy Data, Inc. in 1990, and the company was included in the Inc 500 list of fastest-growing companies in 1995. Galaxy Data specialized in high-speed backbones and Internet security, servicing large companies in the Wisconsin and Chicago market. He sold his share of Galaxy Data to his partner in 1999 and retired.

He spends a lot of time with his grandchildren and volunteers with Big Brothers Big Sisters by mentoring an active eight-year-old boy. Geenen plays tennis and racquetball and sails.